NAMING GOTHAM

The Villains, Rogues
& Heroes Behind
New York's Place Names

REBECCA BRATSPIES

THE
History
PRESS

Published by The History Press
Charleston, SC
www.historypress.com

Front cover, clockwise from top left: Bryant Park, *by Rebecca Bratspies*; Peter Cooper, *Wikimedia Commons*; Henry Bruckner, *Wikimedia Commons*; New York City street scene, *by Thomas Piercy*; Jackie Robinson, *Bob Sandberg, Restoration by Adam Cuerden, public domain, via Wikimedia Commons*; Shirley Chisholm, *public domain, via Library of Congress, LC-U9-25383-33*.

Back cover, top, left to right: Hudson River Vehicular Tunnel, *public domain, via New York Public Library Digital Collections*; NYC street signs, *by Jeffrey Bratspies*; bottom: Pulaski Skyway, *public domain, via Library of Congress, HAER NJ,9-JERCI,10—1*.

Frontispiece: Map of New York City. *By Charlie LaGreca Velasco.*

First published 2023

Manufactured in the United States

ISBN 9781467151405

Library of Congress Control Number: 2022944979

Notice: The information in this book is true and complete to the best of our knowledge. It is offered without guarantee on the part of the author or The History Press. The author and The History Press disclaim all liability in connection with the use of this book.

For New York, the Greatest City in the World

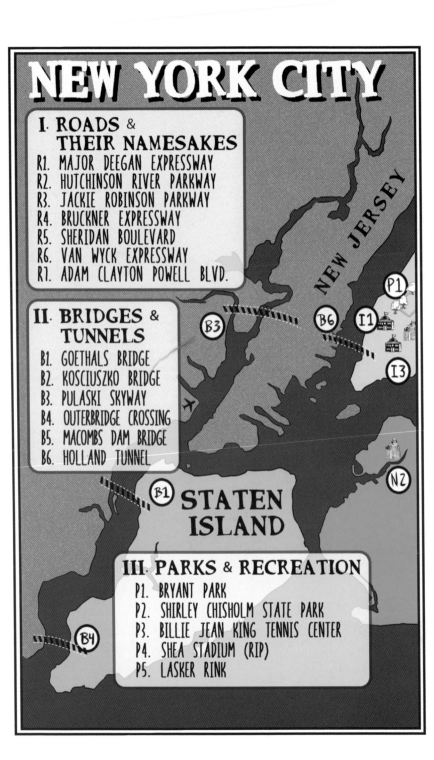

NEW YORK CITY

I. ROADS & THEIR NAMESAKES

R1. MAJOR DEEGAN EXPRESSWAY
R2. HUTCHINSON RIVER PARKWAY
R3. JACKIE ROBINSON PARKWAY
R4. BRUCKNER EXPRESSWAY
R5. SHERIDAN BOULEVARD
R6. VAN WYCK EXPRESSWAY
R7. ADAM CLAYTON POWELL BLVD.

II. BRIDGES & TUNNELS

B1. GOETHALS BRIDGE
B2. KOSCIUSZKO BRIDGE
B3. PULASKI SKYWAY
B4. OUTERBRIDGE CROSSING
B5. MACOMBS DAM BRIDGE
B6. HOLLAND TUNNEL

NEW JERSEY

STATEN ISLAND

III. PARKS & RECREATION

P1. BRYANT PARK
P2. SHIRLEY CHISHOLM STATE PARK
P3. BILLIE JEAN KING TENNIS CENTER
P4. SHEA STADIUM (RIP)
P5. LASKER RINK

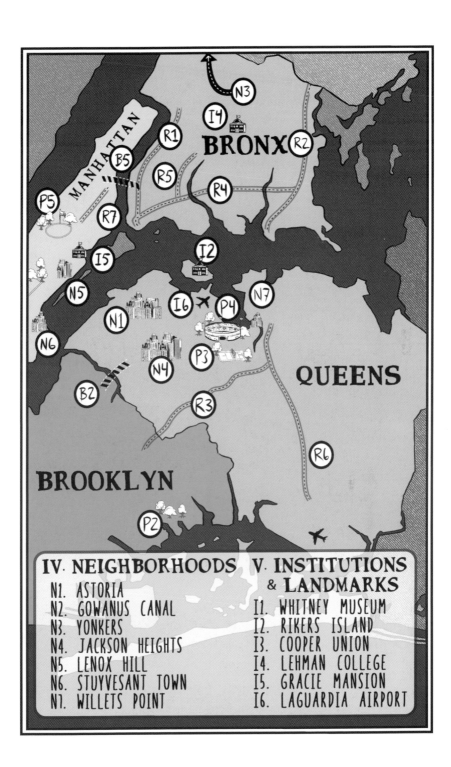

MANHATTAN

BRONX

QUEENS

BROOKLYN

IV. NEIGHBORHOODS

N1. ASTORIA
N2. GOWANUS CANAL
N3. YONKERS
N4. JACKSON HEIGHTS
N5. LENOX HILL
N6. STUYVESANT TOWN
N7. WILLETS POINT

V. INSTITUTIONS & LANDMARKS

I1. WHITNEY MUSEUM
I2. RIKERS ISLAND
I3. COOPER UNION
I4. LEHMAN COLLEGE
I5. GRACIE MANSION
I6. LAGUARDIA AIRPORT

CONTENTS

INTRODUCTION

It is unnecessary to catalogue and argue again, the advantages, natural and artificial, of New York over other cities.[1]

I n New York City, the highways all have designated numbers, just like highways everywhere else in America. But you would never know it from the local traffic reports. Because in New York City, our roads have names. During rush hour, it is not uncommon to hear about an "accident on the Van Wyck," "a disabled vehicle on the Major Deegan" or "a tie-up on the Jackie Robinson."

The Van Wyck, the Major Deegan, the Jackie Robinson, not to mention the Hutch, the Merritt, FDR Drive or the Henry Hudson. You might drive them regularly without really noticing that those road names are, well, names. But who were these people? When did they live? What did they do?

Anyone who drives the Major Deegan Expressway regularly is guaranteed to spend hours stuck in traffic. Depending on the day, it might be Yankees traffic, flooding on the Cross Bronx or just congestion on the George Washington Bridge. Everyone knows George Washington, but who was Major Deegan? Everybody *takes* the Major Deegan, but nobody knows who he was.

Who was that Major Deegan anyway? It became a family joke. Eventually, my husband challenged me to find out. Out of that casual challenge, a hobby was born—finding out about the lives behind the names that adorned so much infrastructure in New York City. Major Deegan was first, but I soon became hooked on this whimsical pathway into the history of the city I love.

New York City's many roads, bridges, neighborhoods and institutions bear the names of a colorful assortment of people from key periods in New York history. Learning about those people is a window into that history—a place-based, more intimate version of history measured on a human scale. This book tells some of those stories.

It was necessarily selective—this book could have been twice as long and still not cover even half of the people who might have been included. My criteria for inclusion had more to do with who caught my fancy than with any defensible historical theory. There are fascinating life stories behind each one of the names that have become New York City's urban shorthand for traffic jams, culture and recreation. Knowing the story behind the name is a way to understanding the City's history—the eras in which these people lived and the struggles and challenges they faced. This book uses those names as a path for considering the history of New York City.

As a result, this book is stuffed with fascinating tidbits. For example, the Outerbridge Crossing was named after Eugenius Outerbridge and is called a crossing because the Outerbridge Bridge sounded absurd; the Bronx derives its name from Dutch settler Jonas Bronck, even though he lived there only for a few years; on the evening Van Wyck was elected, drunks, gamblers and criminals marched through the Tenderloin chanting, "Well, Well, Well, Reform has gone to Hell"; in 1921, thousands of children picketed Bronx Borough president Bruckner demanding that he reduce the cost of ice cream sodas; Kościuszko was an antislavery, anti-serfdom revolutionary; Holland originally thought horse carts would use his eponymous tunnel.

Eventually, the individual stories strung themselves together into a quirky New York City history, one that offered a unique window into urban social structure and the City's ever-changing inhabitants. There are Revolutionary War heroes, robber barons and Tammany Hall politicos—far too many to fit into a single book. Yet those names tell only a small sliver of the City's story. To date, New York City has chosen to commemorate mostly white men. In a city as diverse as New York, that fact is telling. It reflects the historical balance of power in the City—both in terms of who had the power to name things and who got to define what counts as history.

As I was researching and writing this book, that began to change. Statues recognizing a range of Black Americans including Frederick Douglass, Harriet Tubman, Ralph Ellison and Duke Ellington have been dedicated across the City. A statue of women's rights pioneers Sojourner Truth, Elizabeth Cady Stanton and Susan B. Anthony sits in Central Park, and Bryant Park is home to a statue honoring Gertrude Stein. Most significantly, the Shirley Chisholm State Park, named after the first Black woman elected to Congress, opened in 2019. This shift in who the City memorializes reflects the changing narrative that New Yorkers tell themselves about their city. It remains to be seen how this changing story will reverberate in the policies the City adopts for its schools, its roads and its neighborhoods.

Although the names come from many eras, the roads, bridges and structures themselves almost always involve Robert Moses. As planning commissioner, parks commissioner, construction commissioner, arterial coordinator and Triborough Bridge and Tunnel Authority commissioner, Moses spent more than four decades reshaping New York City (and New York State) into an image of his own making. Asked in 1947 to predict the New York of the future, Moses unhesitatingly touted his own work, declaring that "the great arteries of travel will stand out."[2] He boasted that New York City would have a "magnificent modern parkway and expressway system."[3] New York City does have quite a network of major highways—virtually all designed and built by Robert Moses. In various capacities across changing political administrations, Moses was the force behind many of the roads, bridges, parks and public structures described in this book. His choices devastated communities of color and are the reason New York City's mass transit does not reach many neighborhoods.

Over time, I compiled information about an ever-wider swath of New York figures. I kept hearing, "you should write a book about this." So, I did.

ACKNOWLEDGEMENTS

This book has been a labor of love. It is the product of nearly a decade of archival research, as well as endless conversations with my fellow New York history buffs. For much of that time, the working title was "Who Was That Major Deegan Anyway," reflecting the project's origin story. Thank you to everyone who let me drone on endlessly about Deegan, Kościuszko, Lasker and Outerbridge, among others.

For their thoughtful comments on earlier drafts of the book, I want to thank Nicole Galli, Gabrielle Sellei, Judith Wise, Jeff Tapper, Jonathan Forgash and Professor Andrea McArdle. I particularly want to thank my colleague Sarah Lamdan not only for reading multiple drafts of this book but also for helping me submit FOIA requests and, on one memorable (rainy) day, for joining me at the New York City Municipal Archive in a quest to find Arthur Sheridan's birth records. (Fun fact: on any given day throughout the nineteenth and twentieth centuries, many, many people with the last name of Sheridan have had babies in New York City.)

I am grateful to Kathy Williams, Jonathan Saxon and Yasmin Sokkar-Harker for helping me find obscure newspaper articles, images and other materials. Thanks to Dr. Steven Payne at the Bronx County Historical Society Research Library, Ken Cobb at the New York City Municipal Archive and Megan Scauri at the American Jewish Historical Society for helping me locate some hard-to-find photographs and to Hadassah, the Bronx County Historical Society, the Brooklyn Library, the Winterthur Museum, Garden & Library, Back Creek Books, Isobel Ellis, David Pirmann, Heritage Auction,

Rutgers University Library Special Collections and Archives and the Cooper Union Archives for generously allowing me to use their photographs.

Portions of the section on Rikers Island first appeared in my testimony before New York City Council on Renewable Rikers, in *Loyola Law Review* as "Renewable Rikers: A Plan for Restorative Environmental Justice," and in *The Nature of Cities* as "Renewable Rikers as a Blueprint for a Sustainable City."

I have tested many of the stories in this book during presentations at different institutions over the years. I want to particularly thank participants of the AALS 2018 panel on "The Never-Ending Assault on the Administrative State?" for listening to a test run of materials about Samuel Seabury's investigation of corruption in New York City and participants at the 2018 Chicago-Kent Law School symposium on "The Trump Administration and Administrative Law" for their feedback on New York's response to the Fugitive Slave Act.

Thanks to my family for their support in this process—to my father for reading multiple drafts and for driving around New York City with me to take photographs, and to my mother for her endless support. Thank you to my son Sam Schulz for writing the back cover text—I only wish I could write as well as you do. By the way, you are right; I do have a crush on Kościuszko. Thanks to my husband, Allen Schulz, for reading multiple drafts, for listening to endless monologues and for starting me on this path by daring me to find out who Major Deegan was. Special thanks to artist Charlie LaGreca Velasco, my collaborator in the Environmental Justice Chronicles, for creating the map at the front of this book virtually overnight.

This book is dedicated to New York City—the most diverse place on earth and forever "the City" no matter where I am in the world. As I am finishing this book, New York City is emerging from the COVID-19 pandemic. I hope that as we move forward, we will not forget the mutual aid that sprang up spontaneously all over the City in those hellish early days full of sirens and illness. There is so much that is good and right here, and yet we still have much more work to do. Together we can build a better, fairer, more equitable and greener city. The way to start is by remembering our past. We got this!

PART I

ROADS AND THEIR NAMESAKES

Chapter 1

MAJOR DEEGAN

THE LOYAL SIDEKICK

The Major Deegan Expressway was named for William Francis Deegan (December 28, 1882–April 3, 1932).

FAMILY LIFE

Major Deegan was one of five children born in New York City to William F. and Bridget (Maloney) Deegan. As a young man, Deegan studied architecture at the Cooper Institute (*see entry on Peter Cooper*). He had a successful private career before entering public service.

In 1909, Deegan married Violet Secort. The couple had one son, also named William F. Deegan. The marriage did not last long. Violet soon eloped with Deegan's close friend and fellow architect Albert Crouch.[4] At the time they eloped, Crouch was married with three children. After an extensive police hunt, Crouch was arrested in California for abandoning his family (they did that back then). New York City sent two sheriffs to bring Crouch back to New York

Portrait of Major Deegan. *Courtesy of the Municipal Archives, City of New York.*

City, where he faced charges for deserting his family. Crouch was convicted of desertion and ordered to pay $175 in monthly alimony.[5] The Deegans and the Crouches then had a very public, very scandalous joint divorce proceeding. Reportedly, Albert and Violet married immediately afterward.

MILITARY SERVICE

During World War I, Deegan served in the U.S. Army Corps of Engineers under General George Goethals (*see entry on Goethals*). Even though Deegan used his military rank for the rest of his life, he did not see active service during the war. Instead, he put his architectural training to use supervising the construction of army bases in and around New York.

After the war, Deegan helped form the American Legion. In 1921, Deegan was overwhelmingly elected the state commander of the New York American Legion Chapter.[6] In that capacity, Major Deegan personally lobbied President Harding for new veterans' hospitals, successfully persuading the president to construct three new hospitals around New York.[7] Deegan's growing reputation as an advocate for veterans prompted New York City mayor John Hylan to appoint Deegan to the Mayor's Unemployment Commission. Deegan again proved himself a fierce advocate for disabled veterans, pushing businesses to hire ex-servicemen,[8] the City to provide housing and the Veterans Bureau to offer better treatment at medical facilities.[9]

The next year, Major Deegan sought to build on his victories by running for national chairman of the American Legion. One major platform of his campaign was that the Veterans Bureau should immediately fire "all married women…who have husbands able to support [them]" so that their jobs could "be filled by widows or mothers of servicemen who made the ultimate sacrifice."[10]

Although Deegan was initially projected to win the election handily, he wound up losing in an ugly conference fight. Still smarting from Deegan's advocacy over the poor condition of its medical facilities, the Veterans Bureau opposed his nomination and used Deegan's lack of overseas fighting experience to doom his candidacy.[11]

POLITICAL LIFE

Upon losing the American Legion election, Deegan entered local politics. He was handily elected chair of the Bronx Chamber of Commerce. In 1928, Deegan resigned noisily from this position when the chamber voted to sue New York City mayor Jimmy Walker (one of Major Deegan's closest friends)[12] over the Interborough Rapid Transit's (IRT) plan to raise subway fares. In a dispute that became known as the "seven-cent fare fight,"[13] the IRT proposed raising subway fares from five cents per ride to seven cents. However, the IRT's contract with the City explicitly guaranteed a five-cent fare. In 1929, the seven-cent fare fight went all the way to the United States Supreme Court. The court sided with the City, finding that the IRT was contractually barred from raising its fare.

After Deegan resigned from the Chamber of Commerce, Mayor Walker appointed him Tenement House Commissioner, a position akin to today's buildings commissioner. In this role, Deegan was tasked with enforcing the Tenement Act, which established many of the minimum standards for housing that we still live with today: running water and toilets, eight-foot ceilings, fire escapes and hallways illuminated at night.[14]

Commissioner Deegan immediately began making waves. He sent inspectors into buildings across the City and uncovered tens of thousands of landlord violations.[15] Within a year, Deegan was testifying about lax enforcement of fire regulations before the Seabury Commission, the New York legislative committee investigating corruption in Mayor Walker's administration.[16] The Seabury Commission recommended that Walker be removed from office for "gross improprieties and other instances of political malfeasance." In 1932, Walker resigned, decrying the unfair proceedings against him, and announced his intention to "seek vindication with the

Seven-cent fare token. *Courtesy of George Cuhaj/nycsubway.org.*

FUN FACT Confident it would win the lawsuit, the IRT ordered new tokens. After the Supreme Court ruled against them, the IRT was left with six million useless seven-cent tokens. The next year, President Hoover appointed the IRT's lawyer, Charles Hughes, to be Chief Justice of the Supreme Court.

people."[17] Instead, Walker almost immediately moved to Paris with his longtime girlfriend, actress Betty Compton.[18] Walker ultimately became the head of Majestic Records.

Untouched by the scandal, Major Deegan stayed on in city government. In addition to his post as tenement commissioner, Deegan also served as chair of the Mayor's Committee for Welcoming Distinguished Guests, basically the City's official greeter. However, the multiple jobs appeared to be too much for Deegan, and he collapsed from overwork. He was widely rumored to have suffered a heart attack, but doctors characterized Deegan as "on the verge of a nervous breakdown."[19]

Major Deegan died in 1932 at the age of forty-nine due to complications from an appendectomy. His funeral drew more than 3,000 mourners. In addition to military bands, airplane escorts and a caisson drawn by seven black horses, there were 160 honorary pallbearers, including Mayor Walker, two United States senators and a veritable who's who of New York City government.[20] At a time when New York City was rife with corrupt politicians who enriched themselves at the expense of the City, Deegan left a relatively modest estate of less than $10,000.

FUN FACT Deegan may have lacked overseas fighting experience but not overseas travel experience. In 1927, Deegan accompanied Mayor Walker to Paris as Walker's "military aide." Upon their return, Deegan insisted that Walker had been so exhausted by a rigorous work schedule that he had not had any time for Paris's nightlife—a statement directly at odds with press reports about "Beau James's" penchant for lavish evenings, including visits to Josephine Baker's nightclub.*

---

* Paris Gives Walker a Hearty Welcome, N.Y. Times (September 14, 1927); Paris Sees Walker at Grave Ceremony and in Gay Scenes, N.Y. Times (Sept. 15, 1927).

On April 30, 1937, Mayor Fiorello LaGuardia (*see entry on LaGuardia*) signed a city council ordinance renaming the road connecting the Triborough Bridge and the Grand Concourse in the Bronx as Major William F. Deegan Boulevard. A plaque at 138th Street in the Bronx reads, "This boulevard is dedicated to the memory of Major William F. Deegan, QMC, USA. Patriot, Leader, Public Official 1882–1932. Lived in the Service of his fellow man; died in the service of his City."

In the run-up to the 1940 World's Fair held in Flushing Meadows, Queens, Robert Moses began expanding and widening Major Deegan Boulevard.[21] In 1956, the Major Deegan Expressway officially opened. Today, the Major Deegan is Interstate 87, a six-lane highway that runs for 8.5 miles along the Bronx side of the Harlem River, connecting the Triborough Bridge to

Major Deegan Expressway. *Wikimedia Commons.*

the New York Thruway. More than 150,000 vehicles use the Major Deegan each day.

In the fall of 2021, flooding from Hurricane Ida trapped dozens of vehicles in rising waters and raised concerns that the Major Deegan was too vulnerable to climate change. In response, New York City began an ambitious green infrastructure project to daylight the long-buried Tibbets stream—a sustainability move that should significantly reduce flooding on the Major Deegan.

Chapter 2

ANNE HUTCHINSON

THE RADICAL PROPHET

T he Hutchinson Parkway was named for Anne Hutchinson (1591–1643), arguably the most famous woman in colonial America and a pioneer for religious freedom.

EARLY LIFE

Born in Lincolnshire, England, in 1591, Anne was the daughter of Francis and Bridget (Dryden) Marbury. Her father was an outspoken English minister who often clashed with the religious orthodoxy of the Anglican Church. He sent Anne to Oxford, a rarity for girls in those days. In 1612, twenty-one-year-old Anne married William Hutchinson. She and her husband were followers of John Cotton, a charismatic Puritan preacher. By 1633, religious persecution against Puritans had increased in England, and John Cotton immigrated to the Massachusetts Bay Colony. The next year, Hutchinson, her husband and their eleven children followed Cotton to America. On the trip, Hutchinson began getting into trouble for her own religious views, which differed from Puritan orthodoxy.

THEOLOGY

In Boston, Hutchinson worked as a midwife and hosted religious discussion groups for women in her home. A charismatic healer, Hutchinson gained

Anne Hutchinson on Trial, by Edwin Austin Abbey. *Wikimedia Commons.*

renown for her "gift of fluent and inspired speech."[22] The discussions she hosted became immensely popular, and soon men began to attend as well as women. Hutchinson rapidly became an influential religious thinker in the colony, shedding her socially expected role as a modest, submissive and obedient female.[23] However, her religious ideas clashed with those embraced by Boston's Puritan clergy. For example, she claimed that God communicated with her by direct revelations and that she was capable of interpreting the Scriptures on her own. At the time, this was a shocking assertion—one that put Hutchinson in direct conflict with the Puritan tenet that only duly authorized ministers could interpret the Bible.

The religious establishment was further outraged by Hutchinson's claim of an individual relationship with God unmediated by the church. Hutchinson also directly contradicted official Puritan theology by suggesting that salvation was rooted in grace rather than in good works. Finally, Hutchinson's refusal to be subordinate to men undermined entrenched gender roles that dictated that male clergy, and men in general, were at all times superior to mere women. Threatened by Hutchinson's growing popularity, church officials began calling Hutchinson's view antinomian (meaning anti-law).[24] They grew afraid that her influence was encouraging women to assert themselves, thereby jeopardized the stability of the colony.

RELIGIOUS PERSECUTION

In November 1637, newly elected governor John Winthrop ordered Hutchinson's arrest on the charge of "transducing the ministers," basically a charge of sedition. She was brought before the General Court, the colony's principal governing body, to defend herself not only against that allegation but also against the social transgression of being an "American Jezebel"[25] who was "more bold than a man."[26] In her trial, Hutchinson, who was forty-six and pregnant with her sixteenth child, faced off against the colony's leaders.[27] Likening herself to Daniel in the lion's den, Hutchinson matched her inquisitors verse for verse when they accused her of defying scripture[28] and prophesized her own redemption.[29] Outraged by Hutchinson's temerity in "stepping out of place," the ministers accused Hutchinson of promiscuity and of recklessly endangering civic order, insinuating that she was in league with the devil.[30] They convicted her and exiled Hutchinson from the Massachusetts colony as "a woman not fit for our society."[31] The next year, a religious trial resulted in Hutchinson's excommunication. At this proceeding, her former mentor, John Cotton, joined the crowd denouncing Hutchinson. But many of her female followers remained loyal and continued to speak up even after Hutchinson was banished, most notably Mary Dyer, who literally took Hutchinson's hand and escorted her out of the church after her excommunication.

With the encouragement of Roger Williams, who had been banished from the Massachusetts Bay Colony three years earlier, Hutchinson and her followers moved to Rhode Island in 1638. There they established the town of Portsmouth on land purchased from the Narragansett. Unfortunately, Hutchinson's refuge in Rhode Island proved brief. When Massachusetts threatened to invade Rhode Island, Hutchinson was forced to move again. She and her followers, including the six youngest of her fifteen children, moved south to Pelham Bay, which was then part of Dutch New Netherlands and is now part of the Bronx.

In 1643, Hutchinson's settlement was attacked by a Siwanoy band during the conflict known as Kieft's War, after the director-general of New Netherlands. Hutchinson and most of her family were killed in the conflict. Her youngest daughter, Susanna, survived the attack and was ultimately ransomed by the Dutch. Some of Hutchinson's enemies among the Massachusetts clergy expressed satisfaction at her demise, interpreting her violent death as a divine judgment on her heretical theology. Governor Winthrop is reputed to have said, "Proud Jezebel has at last been cast down."[32]

In *The Scarlet Letter*, Nathaniel Hawthorne draws comparisons between his protagonist, Hester Prynne, and Anne Hutchinson, and scholars have suggested that Arthur Dimmesdale is a stand-in for Hutchinson's mentor-turned-critic John Cotton.[33] In an earlier essay titled "Mrs. Hutchinson," Hawthorne wrote sympathetically about Hutchinson as an extraordinary woman who challenged a male-dominated, autocratic society.

HUTCHINSON RIVER PARKWAY

Hutchinson River Parkway shield. *Freddie, Wikimedia Commons.*

The Hutchinson River Parkway, commonly called "the Hutch," is an eighteen-mile stretch of road connecting the Bruckner Expressway (*see entry on Bruckner*) in the Bronx with the Merritt Parkway at the New York–Connecticut border. It runs along the Hutchinson River, a freshwater stream in the Bronx, and forms the border between multiple Westchester towns and suburbs. At the instigation of Robert Moses, the Hutch was built between 1924 and 1941 to "smooth flow of traffic" and promote "desirable residential growth."

Although the original design included bridle paths alongside the road, the Hutch was part of a network of parkways built across New York City for automobile traffic. These parkways were intended to be scenic, with attention to light, air, recreation and aesthetics.[34] During the housing shortage after World War II, these parkways spurred development of suburbs in Westchester and Long Island. Federally insured mortgages available only to returning white GIs and overtly racist deed restrictions kept these new housing developments from being racially integrated. Moses's design reinforced this racism. His parkways, including the Hutch, were designed with multiple stone arch bridges too low for trucks and buses. According to biographer Robert Caro, Moses did this intentionally in order to prevent low-income New Yorkers traveling by bus from reaching certain "desirable" destinations.[35]

Built with the weekend recreational driver in mind, the Hutch was not designed for weekday commuting. By 1953, the Hutch was already considered inadequate for the traffic it bore, with deficient shoulders, narrow lanes and steep hairpin curves. Repeated expansion attempts were rejected because of community concerns about noise, pollution and increased congestion. Reconstruction plans were finally introduced in the late 1990s and were implemented over the next decade. Today, the Hutchinson River Parkway is part of Interstate 678 and handles approximately 150,000 vehicles per day.

FUN FACT
In 1987, to mark the 350th anniversary of her trial, then–Massachusetts governor Michael Dukakis pardoned Hutchinson and revoked her banishment. Today, the United Church of Christ counts Anne Hutchinson as one of its founders.

Chapter 3

JACKIE ROBINSON

THE BARRIER BREAKER

T he Jackie Robinson Parkway was named after Jack Roosevelt Robinson (January 31, 1919–October 24, 1972), the first Black man to play Major League professional baseball.

FAMILY LIFE

Jack Roosevelt Robinson was born in 1919 in Georgia. His parents, Jerry and Mallie (McGriff) Robinson, were struggling sharecroppers. Jerry abandoned the family soon after Jackie was born, and Mallie moved her family across the country to join a brother in Pasadena in search of a better life. As a result, Robinson grew up in California in a mostly white neighborhood where he and his siblings frequently faced racial harassment. Robinson attended Pomona Junior College and UCLA. From an early age, Robinson showed exceptional athletic prowess. He was a champion tennis player, a medal-winning track star and a baseball and football star. During his time at UCLA, he became the first athlete to win varsity letters in four sports: baseball, basketball, football and track.

Jackie Robinson. Photo by Bob Sandberg, restoration by Adam Cuerden. *Wikimedia Commons.*

In 1946, Robinson married Rachel Isum. Together, they had three children.

Military Service

After the Japanese bombed Pearl Harbor, Robinson was drafted into the segregated army and stationed at Fort Riley in Kansas. Robinson applied to Officer Candidate School. Despite his having the necessary qualifications, it took significant wrangling and the personal intervention of Heavyweight Champion Joe Lewis to get Robinson and other qualified Black soldiers admitted. In 1943, Robinson was commissioned a second lieutenant.

Jackie Robinson military photo. *Library of Congress.*

Robinson's time in the army wound up being short-lived. The very next year, while stationed at Camp Hood, Texas, Robinson was arrested by military police for a dispute that broke out after Robinson refused to move to the back of a military bus. While Texas was a segregated state, segregation was prohibited on military buses, so Robinson was well within his legal rights to refuse. The bus driver, and later one of the MPs, called Robinson an insulting racial epithet, and things escalated from there. Despite being the victim, it was Robinson who wound up arrested, handcuffed and shackled. Robinson soon found himself facing a court-martial for alleged insubordination toward the officer in charge, a captain named Gerald M. Bear. Robinson's case was heard by a jury of nine officers, eight of whom were white. He was charged with two counts: "behaving with disrespect toward a superior officer" and "willful disobedience of a lawful command" from a superior officer. Robinson's commander at Camp Hood, Lieutenant Colonel Paul Bates, testified glowingly on his behalf, and Robinson took the stand in his own defense.[36] Robinson was acquitted on both counts and soon after received an honorable discharge.

Baseball Career

After leaving the military, Robinson joined the Kansas City Monarchs, an all-Black baseball team playing in the segregated Negro League. After one season with the Monarchs, Branch Rickey famously approached Robinson about joining the Brooklyn Dodgers. For decades, Major League Baseball team owners had honored a so-called gentlemen's agreement to exclude

FUN FACT Jackie wasn't the only athlete in the family. His older brother Mack Robinson won a silver medal in the 200 meters at the 1936 Berlin Olympics (the Nazi Olympics), finishing 0.4 seconds behind Jesse Owens. Upon his return to Pasadena, the only job that silver medalist Mack Robinson could find was as a janitor.

Black players. However, the New York legislature had recently enacted the Ives-Quinn Act, which made it unlawful for a New York employer to refuse to hire a person because of race, color, religion or national origin. Major League Baseball was incorporated in New York and thus subject to this law. New York City mayor Fiorello LaGuardia (*see entry on LaGuardia*) established a committee to study racial discrimination in baseball. The committee, whose members included Branch Rickey, issued a report characterizing segregation in baseball as "sheer prejudice" and called on Major League Baseball to take responsibility for ending segregation in baseball. In 1945, Rickey signed Robinson to play for the Dodgers.

As a Dodger, Robinson would be the first Black player in the National League—ending decades of racial segregation in baseball. Both Rickey and Robinson knew that there would be ugliness and confrontation ahead. Rickey demanded that Robinson promise not to respond to the racial abuse that would be directed his way. The Dodgers signed Robinson only after he committed to "turn the other cheek." In a newspaper column he wrote about his contract, Robinson made it clear that he knew he carried the weight of the country's fifteen million Black citizens on his shoulders, writing, "I will not forget that I am representing a whole race of people who are pulling for me."[37]

Robinson first played a season with the Montreal Royals, a farm team. There, Robinson excelled, leading the league in batting and coming in second in stolen bases. With him on the team, the Royals won the Minor League championship. But it had not been easy. Robinson faced insult after insult from racist fans. The next year, Rickey moved spring training to Cuba to avoid Jim Crow segregation.

On April 15, 1947, Robinson "broke the color barrier" when he made his major-league debut with the Brooklyn Dodgers at Ebbets Field. Over the course of his first year in the Major Leagues, Robinson faced racial slurs hurled at him by opposing players and fans and even racially charged hostility from his own teammates. Despite the harassment, Robinson played remarkable baseball, helping the Dodgers win the pennant. By the end of that year, Robinson was the second most popular person in America, behind Bing Crosby but ahead of President Harry S. Truman and General Dwight D. Eisenhower.[38]

Jackie Robinson Congressional Medal of Honor, United States Mint. *Design, obverse*: Donna Weaver. *Reverse*: John Mercanti. Reverse sculpted by Don Everhart. *Wikimedia Commons.*

Jackie Robinson Parkway. *Photo by Rebecca Bratspies.*

In 1947, Robinson received Major League Baseball's first Rookie of the Year Award. Two years later, he was named the National League's Most Valuable Player. He was an All-Star from 1949 to 1954 and played in six World Series. He played 162 games, averaging 16 runs per season.[39] In 1962, Robinson was inducted into the Baseball Hall of Fame.

After retiring from baseball, Robinson continued to break barriers, becoming the first Black person to serve as vice president of a major American corporation (Chock Full O' Nuts). He wrote a regular column for the *New York Post* and the *Amsterdam News*. Despite suffering from heart disease and diabetes, Robinson remained active in politics and civil rights until his death in 1972 at age fifty-three. In 2005, Robinson was posthumously awarded a Congressional Medal of Honor for his "exceptional fortitude and integrity."[40]

After his death, Rachel Robinson founded the Jackie Robinson Development Corporation and the Jackie Robinson Foundation. The Development Corporation specializes in low- and moderate-income housing, and the foundation provides scholarships to minority students.

In May 1997, to commemorate the fiftieth anniversary of Robinson integrating baseball, New York City renamed the Interboro Parkway the Jackie Robinson Parkway. The Jackie Robinson Parkway is a five-mile stretch of road connecting Jamaica Avenue in Brooklyn with the Grand Central and the Van Wyck in Queens. More than 82,000 vehicles use the Jackie Robinson each day.[41]

FUN FACT In 1997, Major League Baseball officially retired no. 42, Jackie Robinson's uniform number. On Jackie Robinson Day, held each year on April 15 to commemorate the day Robinson made his major-league debut, all the players on both teams, as well as the coaches, managers and umpires, wear no. 42 on their jerseys.

Chapter 4

HENRY BRUCKNER

THE SODAPOP KING

T he Bruckner Expressway is named after Bronx borough president Henry Bruckner (1871–1942).

FAMILY LIFE

Henry Bruckner was born in the Bronx on June 17, 1871, to parents John A. and Katharine (Schmidt) Bruckner. He attended New York City public schools, graduating from PS 62 in 1886. With his brother John, Henry founded Bruckner Bros. Beverages in 1892. Their endeavor was wildly successful, and within a short period, Bruckner Bros. had grown into New York City's largest soda water bottler. In 1904, Bruckner married Helen Zobel. Together, they had three sons: Henry Jr., William and Jack. Helen died young, and her 1930 funeral was a political affair, with New York City mayor Jimmy Walker and Major Deegan among those in attendance.

Henry Bruckner. *Wikimedia Commons.*

POLITICAL CAREER

* The Uses of Adversity, American Bottler, Vol. 37 p. 37 (Jan. 15, 1917).

Bruckner began his political career by running for the New York state legislature in 1900. During the course of the election, Bruckner was glowingly endorsed by the *Tammany Times* as a universally liked candidate "whose word was as good as his bond."[42] Nevertheless, after winning the election to represent New York County's Thirty-Fifth District in the State Assembly, Bruckner almost immediately abandoned his constituents. He resigned one year into his term in order to accept an appointment as the Bronx Commissioner of Public Works, a position he held for eleven years (1901–12).

Bruckner left the Public Works Commission to run for Congress on the Tammany ticket. He represented the New York Twenty-Second Congressional District from 1913 to 1917. Bruckner served two full terms in Congress, during which he was a member of the Committee of Public Buildings and the Merchant Marine Committee and chaired the House Railway and Canal Committee. While in Congress, Bruckner missed 53 percent of the roll call votes.[43] Bruckner resigned from Congress in 1917 to run for Bronx borough president. As part of an ugly campaign, then–New York City mayor John Mitchel impugned Bruckner's patriotism, characterizing him as a German sympathizer. Mitchel asserted that Bruckner's election would degrade the Bronx by demonstrating that the borough was disloyal. Bruckner nevertheless won the election and served as Bronx Borough president for the next fifteen years, from 1918 to 1933.

Throughout his political career, Bruckner continued running his bottling company, now known as Bruckner Beverages. Indeed, just months after leaving Congress, Bruckner was back in Washington, testifying before the House Ways and Means Committee in opposition to a proposed five-cent sugar tax that Bruckner claimed would have doubled the cost of his soda.[44] His best-known brand, U-No-Us, was very popular during Prohibition. In 1921, Bruckner registered U-No-Us as a United States trademark.[45] At the time, the flavors sold under the brand included ginger ale, birch beer, lemon and artificial raspberry sarsaparilla.

CORRUPTION SCANDAL

A staunch Tammany Hall Democrat, Bruckner had close ties to Mayor Jimmy Walker and the Tammany political machine. That meant that Bruckner was swept up in the corruption investigations instituted by the New York legislature and led by Judge Samuel Seabury. In 1932, Seabury summoned Bruckner to appear under oath and testify about the large sum of money he had accumulated while serving as Bronx Borough president. Seabury wanted to know details about Bruckner's eight bank accounts, $276,000 in bank deposits and the multiple safety-deposit boxes that Bruckner and his son had visited 185 times over a five-year period.[46] Following the September 1, 1932 resignation of Mayor Jimmy Walker, Judge Seabury urged that Bruckner be removed from his position as Bronx Borough president, on the ground that "his neglect and incompetence was apparent."[47] A more generous but equally damning description of Bruckner's time in office was that "[h]e made no ripples....The job, at that point, just kind of asked you to sit on your hands and do nothing. And that's what he did."[48]

Seabury also called for the removal of Bruckner's chief aide, public works commissioner William J. Flynn.[49] Flynn had been much more in the corruption investigation crosshairs than had Bruckner. Indeed, there were multiple allegations that Flynn engaged in self-dealing and steered public contracts to political friends.[50] Flynn reportedly manipulated the issuance of construction contracts to establish himself as a "virtual dictator of the building trades in the Borough." There is no question he amassed a personal fortune during his time as public works commissioner. Flynn had this opportunity because Bruckner was frequently absent from office, leaving Flynn as acting borough president. In 1921, for example, Bruckner was diagnosed with "sleeping sickness," which prompted a month-long furlough from office.

Bruckner refused to resign or to exercise his power to remove Flynn, stating, "As long as I am satisfied with the way Commissioner Flynn does his work—and I am—I do not see any reason why I should remove him."[51] Both Governor Franklin Roosevelt and

FUN FACT Bruckner sold his soda water for fifteen to twenty cents a bottle. In 1921, one thousand New York City children marched on Bronx Borough Hall to protest the high cost of ice cream sodas. The protesters carried signs calling on Bruckner to reduce the cost of soda to a nickel.* Today, empty Bruckner Bros. bottles sell for roughly fifteen dollars on eBay.

_____

* Bronx Youth Demand Nickel Soda: Thousands March to Enforce "Rights," N.Y. Times (Jul. 10, 1921).

Acting Mayor Joseph McKee declined to remove Bruckner from office. Nevertheless, Bruckner's thirty-three-year political career ended the next year when Bronx Democratic Party boss Edward J. Flynn (no relation to William Flynn) refused to support his reelection bid.

Bruckner died of kidney disease on April 14, 1942. He was seventy years old. To the end, Bruckner remained extremely popular. Indeed, one thousand people, including Mayor Fiorello LaGuardia (*see entry on LaGuardia*), attended his funeral.[52]

BRUCKNER EXPRESSWAY

Bruckner Expressway sign.
Courtesy of Jeffrey Bratspies.

Several months after Bruckner's death, city council voted to rename Eastern Boulevard, a major Bronx thoroughfare, Bruckner Boulevard in his honor. A decade later, Robert Moses transformed Bruckner Boulevard into the Bruckner Expressway, an elevated highway connecting the Major Deegan with the New England Expressway. Moses routed the Bruckner through the heart of the Soundview neighborhood, a choice fiercely opposed by residents still reeling from construction of the Cross Bronx Expressway through their neighborhood. Moses prevailed, and his highway further devastated the community. Sandwiched between the Cross Bronx, the Major Deegan and the Bruckner, the South Bronx has some of the highest childhood asthma rates in the country.

Today, the Bruckner Expressway, designated I-278, carries 117,000 vehicles per day, including approximately 400 trucks per hour.

Chapter 5

ARTHUR V. SHERIDAN

THE PROFESSIONAL ENGINEER

The Sheridan Expressway was named after Arthur Vincent Sheridan (1887–1952), an engineer who worked closely with Robert Moses to design and build many of New York City's major highways.

A native New Yorker, Sheridan was born on November 24, 1887 (or 1888—he used both dates), to parents Francis J. and Elizabeth (McLaughlin) Sheridan. He was one of two sons. Sheridan attended City College and studied engineering at Columbia University, as well as the Sorbonne. In 1907, he applied and was appointed to be a topographical draughtsman for the City of New York.[53]

Arthur V. Sheridan.
Courtesy of the Bronx County Historical Society Research Library.

He served overseas for two years in the American Expeditionary Force during World War I in both engineer and infantry units, receiving an honorable discharge in April 1919.[54] Upon his return from the war, Sheridan took up a position as an assistant engineer for the Bronx. Unsatisfied with his salary, Sheridan petitioned the City for a raise, arguing that he should get the higher salary paid to those who passed an exam he had missed while serving overseas. He received his raise by virtue of a City Resolution personally directed at him by name. His new annual salary was $4,010[55] ($47,400 in 2015 dollars). By 1927, Sheridan was advocating for increased pay for engineers more widely.[56]

In 1939, Sheridan married Dorothy Catherine Kozneski. He was fifty-three, and she was twenty-one. Together, they had one son, Arthur V. Sheridan Jr. Their May–December marriage did not last long. By 1946, Dorothy had obtained a divorce in Florida.

Working in the Bronx

In 1934, Bronx Borough president James Lyons named Sheridan chief engineer of the Bronx. In that capacity, Sheridan oversaw part of the Triborough Bridge construction, a project that evicted tens of thousands of people from their Bronx neighborhood homes.[57] Four years later, Mayor LaGuardia appointed Sheridan to the City Planning Commission, in which capacity he began working closely with Robert Moses. In 1942, Sheridan stepped down from the City Planning Commission and was appointed as the Bronx commissioner of public works, a position he held for the next decade until his death. Sheridan got the post in part because he was nonpartisan—a welcome change from Robert L. Moran, the office's prior incumbent, who had been ensnared in the scandals that brought down Bronx Borough president Henry Bruckner (*see entry on Bruckner*).[58] Sheridan served as acting borough president in 1946.

Sheridan was a specialist in municipal engineering and high-speed highway design. In the months preceding the United States' entry into World War II, he expressed concern that the streets and highways of New York were unequal to the needs of high-speed wartime transportation.[59] Since he was on the City Planning Commission at the time, his words carried real weight. A few years earlier, while representing the United States at the 1938 International Housing and Town Planning Congress, Sheridan had warned that New York was vulnerable to air attack, particularly its subway system.[60] When the United States entered the Second World War, Sheridan served as a consultant to the army.

During his decade as Bronx commissioner of public works, Sheridan was a staunch ally of New York City arterial coordinator Robert Moses.[61] Sheridan and Moses worked closely to

FUN FACT In his capacity as Bronx commissioner of public works, Sheridan tried to persuade the U.S. Army Corps of Engineers to give the Bronx River "the French touch" by building piers and quays similar to those that line the Seine in Paris.*

---

* Army Urged to Remodel Bronx River to Look Like Seine, with Walls and Quays, N.Y. Times (Feb. 14, 1946).

oversee construction of the Cross-Bronx Expressway and the Major Deegan Expressway. Tens of thousands of Bronx residents were dislocated to make way for these projects, which Mayor LaGuardia (*see entry on LaGuardia*) lauded as a "slum clearance" effort as well as a major public work project.

PROFESSIONAL ENGINEER

Sheridan was a founding member of the National Society of Professional Engineers and served as the organization's second president (1937–38).[62] He was the longtime editor of the society's journal, *The American Engineer*. Sheridan also founded the Association of Engineers of New York, serving as its president, as well as president of its successor organization, the New York State Society of Engineers. His ambition was to create a professional engineering organization on par with the lawyers' bar association,[63] in part to stave off unionization. Indeed, Sheridan gave speeches asserting that the CIO posed a danger to engineers' "integrity and identity."[64] He urged that engineers ally themselves with doctors, lawyers and other "professional men" to combat the danger of unions. Sheridan also was a prominent voice calling on the federal government to establish a Department of Public Works as a cabinet-level position.[65] The post would be filled, naturally, by a professional engineer.

Sheridan was honored by the National Society of Professional Engineers for his contributions to engineering.[66] He wrote numerous books on engineering, including *Whither Engineering Education?* and *Traffic in the Bronx*.[67] Over the years, Sheridan taught engineering at the Stevens Institute, NYU and Manhattan College. In 1942, Manhattan College awarded Sheridan its first ever honorary doctorate of engineering, lauding his accomplishments in "remodeling the city according to the best prescriptions of modern science." To this day, Manhattan College has a tuition assistance grant to needy students named in his honor.[68]

Sheridan, the highway expert, had the most ironic of deaths. He died in a car accident in 1952 at the age of sixty-four. Actually, his death was both grisly and tragic. His car skidded into the path of an oil truck, and Sheridan was decapitated in the accident.[69] He was just days away from retirement.

FUN FACT Sheridan's obituary in *The American Engineer* stated that he had received two presidential commendations for his engineering works: one from President Herbert Hoover and one from Franklin D. Roosevelt. The claim is widely repeated across the internet. However, neither the Herbert Hoover Presidential Library nor the Roosevelt Presidential Library has any record of such a commendation.

SHERIDAN EXPRESSWAY

A city council ordinance renaming the proposed Bronx River Expressway in Sheridan's honor was signed into law by Mayor Vincent R. Impellitteri on February 18, 1953.[70] Construction began in 1958. The $9.5 million Sheridan Expressway, a 1.4-mile-long stub road that connects the Bruckner and Cross Bronx Expressways, opened for traffic on February 6, 1963. At the time, there were plans to extend it northward. However, faced with opposition from Pelham Parkway and Baychester residents, as well as from the nearby Bronx Zoo and New York Botanical Gardens, New York governor Nelson Rockefeller abandoned the plan in 1971.

Sheridan Boulevard sign.
Courtesy of Jeffrey Bratspies.

Local community leaders long argued that the Sheridan Expressway, known as "the highway to nowhere," was superfluous and redundant. Instead, they argued that the Sheridan Expressway should be demolished and converted back into an ordinary street. In 2019, New York City completed the process of dismantling Robert Moses's Sheridan Expressway and replacing it with Sheridan Boulevard, a more modest pedestrian- and bike-friendly road that no longer blocks the access of adjacent neighborhoods to the revitalized Bronx River greenway and its network of parks and paths.[71]

Chapter 6

ROBERT VAN WYCK

THE CORRUPT MAYOR

The Van Wyck Expressway was named after Robert Anderson Van Wyck (1847–1918), mayor of New York from 1891 to 1901. Depending on how you count, Van Wyck was either New York City's ninety-first mayor or its first. He was the ninety-first since the British captured New Amsterdam in 1665 and the first mayor of the City of Greater New York, formed in 1898 by the union of Staten Island, Brooklyn, Manhattan, Queens and the Bronx.

FAMILY LIFE

Van Wyck was born in New York City in 1846 to parents William and Lydia Ann (Maverick) Van Wyck. Both sides of the family were wealthy landholders, the Van Wycks in New York and the Mavericks in South Carolina (where they enslaved dozens of people).

Van Wyck was one of seven children. He spent most of his childhood in South Carolina, where his family socialized with John C. Calhoun, among others, His older brother Augustus, along with another brother, Samuel Maverick Van Wyck, and Van Wyck's brother-in-law Robert Hoke sided with the South during the Civil War and were Confederate officers. The much-younger Van Wyck returned to New York City with his parents, who did not support treason against the Union.

FUN FACT The word *maverick*, meaning "one who does not conform," is an eponym from Van Wyck's maternal uncle Samuel Augustus Maverick, who refused to brand or fence his large Texan cattle herd.

ROBERT ANDERSON VAN WYCK
FIRST MAYOR OF THE CONSOLIDATED CITY OF NEW YORK (1898–1902)

Robert Anderson Van Wyck. *New York Public Library Digital Collection.*

After the war ended, Van Wyck's brother Augustus, known as "a man without hobbies or enthusiasms,"[72] became a major force in New York's Democratic politics and served as a state judge until resigning to run unsuccessfully for governor against Teddy Roosevelt.

Van Wyck moved in elite social circles. He was connected by marriage and kinship with the wealthiest families in old New York. While serving as mayor, he was elected president of the Holland Society, an organization he and his brother Augustus helped found,[73] and was a prominent freemason as a member of Ancient Lodge #724.

A Slimy Political Career

After graduating first in his class from Columbia Law School in 1872, Van Wyck entered politics under the auspices of Tammany Hall (the powerful local political machine) and was elected to a city court judgeship. He was

The Triumph of Van Wyck, by
Homer Davenport. *Library of
Congress.*

rapidly appointed chief judge, a post he resigned to run for mayor in 1897
as Tammany boss Richard Croker's personal choice for the Tammany
Hall ticket.[74] Indeed, Van Wyck was described as "one of Tammany Hall's
worst tools."[75] Nevertheless, he won the election and commenced an
administration that the *New York Times* described as mired in "black ooze
and slime."[76]

THE ICE TRUST SCANDAL

From almost the beginning, the Van Wyck administration was rocked by
scandal. The most notorious was the Ice Trust Scandal, a scheme between
the American Ice Company and various New York City elected officials to
monopolize the City's ice supply and double the price of ice. In the years
before refrigeration, ice was a vital commodity. Entire industries depended
on ice, as did all the restaurants and private homes in the City. A doubling
of ice prices would have made it impossible for the City's millions of poor
immigrants to keep food and medicines from spoiling.

Ice was imported to the City, sometimes from Upstate New York and
sometimes from as far away as Maine. American Ice not only had a monopoly
over the ice supply itself but also managed to obtain the exclusive right to
unload ice at New York City's docks and piers.

Ice Trust *Puck* cover, by Samuel D. Ehrhart. *Wikimedia Commons.*

At roughly the same time that American Ice received exclusive access to New York City docks and piers, Mayor Van Wyck somehow acquired five thousand American Ice shares (valued at more than $680,000 at the time— roughly $12 million in today's dollars) apparently without paying for them. For perspective, Van Wyck, who was not a wealthy man, earned an annual $15,000 salary as mayor.

After obtaining his shares, Van Wyck used his power as mayor to veto a bill that would have increased dock space and thereby allow other companies to compete with American Ice. An investigation led by his fellow Mason (and his brother's old electoral rival) Governor Theodore Roosevelt found no evidence that Van Wyck had engaged in willful wrongdoing, and Roosevelt decided not to use his power as governor to remove Van Wyck from office. Nonetheless, the Ice Trust Scandal doomed Van Wyck's political career.

FUN FACT On the evening Van Wyck was elected mayor, drunken gamblers and petty criminals marched through the Tenderloin district chanting, "Well, Well, Well, Reform has gone to Hell."*

OTHER CORRUPTION SCANDALS

* Milton Mackay, Tin Box Parade 9 (1934).

Van Wyck was also involved in the so-called Ramapo Water Steal. In 1899, New York City granted the Ramapo Water Company a forty-year contract to supply the City with $5 million worth of water per year. The problems: the Ramapo Water Company was a dummy concern, the price was roughly double the going rate for water and the City had no water shortage necessitating the deal. The *New York Times* described the scandal as "one long track and trail of rottenness" and "a bold and infamous scheme of pillage."[77] The contract aroused so much public outrage that the New York legislature intervened and revoked the contract.

A police corruption scandal rounded out Van Wyck's tenure as mayor. As mayor, Van Wyck appointed William Devery to be unified New York City's first police chief in 1898 (Devery was also New York's last police superintendent in 1897). Known as "Big Bill," Devery had a well-deserved reputation for corruption. He was indicted several times for blackmail, extortion and failure to enforce the law. Under Devery, the police department reportedly "chartered vice and controlled graft" in New York City.[78] Mayor Van Wyck described Devery as "the best Chief of Police New York ever had"[79] just twenty days before the New York legislature removed Devery from office over the mayor's veto.

FUN FACT Bill Devery was instrumental in bringing American League Baseball to New York City. Devery became part owner of the team that would ultimately become the New York Yankees.

By the time his single term as mayor was over, Van Wyck had amassed a fortune of $5 million (more than $138 million in today's dollars). The day after he left office, Van Wyck married Katherine Hertle, née Britt, who had divorced her first husband a year earlier. The newlyweds immediately left New York for Paris, where they lived until Van Wyck's death in 1918. In his obituary, the *New York Times* asserted that Van Wyck had been involved in "more administrative scandals than any Mayor in the City's history."[80]

Given his checkered history, you may wonder why New York City decided to name anything in his honor. The answer is that for all his obvious flaws, Van Wyck oversaw a critical moment in New York City history. He managed the integration of New York City into a single political entity, and it was under his watch that construction began on the city's first subway line. In 1900, Van Wyck ceremonially turned the first shovel of earth for what would become the IRT (Interborough Rapid Transit) line between City Hall and 148th Street.

The Van Wyck Expressway

Today, the 9.3-mile section of I-678 that connects JFK Airport to the Grand Central Parkway is known as the Van Wyck Expressway. The Van Wyck opened on October 14, 1950.[81] The roadway was intended to cut travel time

Van Wyck on-ramp sign. *Photo by Rebecca Bratspies.*

between then-Idlewild Airport (now JFK) and midtown Manhattan. During its design and construction, Robert Moses steadily ignored all calls to include rapid transit in the design of the highway. Moses predicted that "traffic will flow freely" along the Van Wyck Expressway.[82] However, within weeks, congestion was so bad that during rush hour the road "resembled a parking lot."[83] Given the "dismal stretch of road"[84] involved, it is perhaps appropriate that the Sanitation Department Band provided the music for the opening ceremony.[85]

To this day, the Van Wyck is a "notorious traffic hazard"[86] with "legendary traffic jams."[87] Nearly 170,000 vehicles use the Van Wyck each day.[88] In 1998, the Port Authority retrofitted the Van Wyck Expressway to remedy Robert Moses's refusal to add mass transit. The Air Train now runs down the middle of a portion of the Van Wyck Expressway, thereby connecting JKF Airport with the New York City subway system at Jamaica. However, traffic jams on the Van Wyck remained a key bottleneck affecting JFK Airport. In 2019, New York approved a $1.2 billion roadway redesign intended to increase capacity on the Van Wyck and improve vehicular travel time to JFK Airport. This work is ongoing.

FUN FACT To the surprise of many New Yorkers, the proper pronunciation of his name is *Van Wike* rather than *Van Wick*.* According to legend, someone once questioned Robert Moses about his pronunciation of the Van Wyck Expressway. His reply: "I'm Robert Moses. I can call it whatever I damn please!"

_____

* Dan Bilefsky, In a Jam on the Van Wyck? Try to Say It Right, N.Y. Times (May 25, 2011).

Chapter 7

ADAM CLAYTON POWELL JR.

MR. CIVIL RIGHTS

A dam Clayton Powell Jr. Boulevard is named after Adam Clayton Powell Jr. (November 29, 1908–April 4, 1972), the first Black New Yorker elected to the House of Representatives.

FAMILY LIFE

Adam Clayton Powell Jr.
*Photo by James J. Kriegsman,
Library of Congress.*

Adam Clayton Powell Jr. was born in New Haven, Connecticut, to parents Mattie Fletcher Schaffer and Adam Clayton Powell Sr. His paternal grandparents, Anthony and Sally Powell, had both been enslaved, and all his life, Powell remembered seeing the large *P* that was branded on his grandfather's back. When Powell was just a baby, Adam Sr. was appointed minister of the Abyssinian Baptist Church, and the family moved to New York City. Under Adam Sr.'s leadership, the Abyssinian Baptist Church grew and prospered, moving to Harlem and becoming one of the largest Protestant congregations in the United States.

Powell attended Townsend Harris High School, an elite public school. Although academically talented, he often struggled socially. After graduating, he attended New York's City College. During his first year, his older sister Blanche died suddenly of a misdiagnosed ruptured appendix.[89] Devastated, Powell dropped out of college and began frequenting the lively nightlife scene of the Harlem Renaissance.

Eager to get his son away from riotous living, Adam Sr. arranged for Powell to attend Colgate University in Hamilton, New York. On campus, Powell was one of five Black students. However, because of his light skin, Powell "passed" as white until his junior year, when Adam Sr. visited Colgate to deliver a lecture about race relations.[90] Newly aware of his Black race, many of Powell's former friends rejected him.[91]

Powell graduated from Colgate in 1930 with a degree in biblical literature. After graduation, Powell followed his father into the ministry and joined the Abyssinian Baptist Church as an assistant minister. He earned a degree in religious studies from Columbia University, and in 1937, Powell took over from his father as head pastor of the Abyssinian Baptist Church.

In 1933, Powell married actress Isabel Washington and adopted her son Preston.[92] Their marriage, the first of three for Powell, did not last long. The couple divorced in 1945, and Powell immediately remarried, this time to Juilliard-trained pianist and movie star Hazel Scott. Powell and Hazel had one child, Adam Clayton Powell III. The couple divorced in 1960, and Powell almost immediately married his secretary Yvette Flores, with whom he had a son named Adam Clayton Powell Diego. Their marriage also ended in divorce.

As a pastor, Powell was deeply involved in political movements in New York City. Everywhere he went, he cut a flamboyant figure, stylish and handsome, rousing crowds with his oratory. He organized strategic, highly visible protests against racial discrimination in hiring, including at the 1939 World's Fair in Flushing Meadows park. The protests produced sweeping changes in hiring practices—ultimately opening doors for Black workers across the City and making Powell a hero in Harlem.

Political Life

In 1941, with the endorsement of Mayor Fiorello LaGuardia (*see entry on LaGuardia*), Powell ran for city council. He won and, at age thirty-three, become city council's first Black member. During his term in office, he continued his advocacy against racially discriminatory hiring practices and co-founded *The People's Voice*, a Harlem-based newspaper for which he served as editor-in-chief. Three years later, Powell ran for Congress—seeking to represent a newly created Harlem district. He conducted a theatrical campaign—the elegantly clad, charismatic Powell rolled up 7th Avenue on a bandwagon and gave rousing speeches whenever it stopped.[93] While his style may have been flashy, the subject of those speeches—racial justice— was deadly serious. Powell handily won the primary on both the Democratic and Republican lines and ran unopposed in the general election. He became the first Black congressman from the Northeast and for many years was one of two Black House members (the other was William Levi Dawson of Illinois).

Adam Clayton Powell Jr. reports. *Wikimedia Commons.*

Powell won reelection twelve times. A charismatic and compelling speaker, he took every opportunity to issue uncompromising calls for racial justice. At a time when few politicians openly supported racial equality, Powell spoke up often and eloquently. His fierce advocacy helped launch the civil rights movement. He was recognized with honorary degrees from two Historically Black Colleges and Universities: Shaw University (divinity) and Virginia Union (law).

As a legislator, Powell was remarkably successful. Early in his career, he repeatedly introduced legislation designed to further social justice, even though he knew it would not be enacted. He attached an anti-discrimination clause to so many pieces of legislation that the rider became known as the "Powell Amendment." Initially purely symbolic, the "Powell Amendment" ultimately became Title VI of the Civil Rights Act, a foundation of equal protection under the law. Powell successfully shepherded many of his other civil rights talking points into legislation—enacting laws that criminalized lynching, dismantled school segregation, promoted worker rights and abolished the poll tax. In 1961, Powell became chair of the Committee on Education and Labor. In that role, he worked closely with both Presidents Kennedy and Johnson to implement wide-ranging social reforms, enacting legislation addressing minimum wages, school lunches, student loans and many other social welfare programs.

Powell's mere presence in the Congress infuriated his more racist colleagues, many of whom were committed to preserving segregation despite a Supreme Court decision declaring "separate but equal" unconstitutional.[94]

During a July 1955 House Education and Labor Committee meeting, West Virginia Democrat Cleveland Bailey punched Powell in the face for proposing that his anti-segregation rider be added to the federal school construction bill. *Brown v. Board of Education*, decided the year before, already outlawed such practices, but Bailey nevertheless accused Powell of "trying to wreck the public school system." Bailey suffered no consequences for his actions. News outlets reported that after much pressure from his fellow representatives, Bailey (the aggressor) agreed to shake hands and "forget the incident."[95] There was no reporting about how Powell felt, but both men later denied that the incident even happened.[96]

Avowed segregationist Missouri representative John E. Rankin declared he would never sit near Powell. In response, Powell made sure to sit as close to Rankin as possible. Once, Powell followed Rankin around the House, moving from seat to seat with him five times.[97] Just weeks into his first term, Powell used his first House speech to condemn Rankin's antisemitism. Powell stated boldly, "Last week democracy was shamed by the uncalled for and unfounded condemnation of one of America's great minorities."[98] Making his commitment to justice and equality clear, Powell continued, "I am not a member of that great minority, but I will always oppose anyone who tries to besmirch any group because of race, creed or color."[99] Powell also denounced the racial slurs frequently uttered in the House by Rankin and other southern Democrats, demanding an inquiry by the House parliamentarian into the use of "disparaging racist terms" on the House floor.[100]

Powell openly defied Washington's segregation laws. He walked boldly into segregated restaurants, daring them to exclude him, and he made sure to use the Capitol facilities that had informal rules excluding Black members.[101] He took Black constituents and his staff to the whites-only House Restaurant. He successfully desegregated the House press galleries. After the Daughters of the American Revolution very publicly invoked their whites-only policy to ban his wife, Hazel, from performing at Constitution Hall, Powell asked President and Mrs. Truman to intervene. They refused. First Lady Bess Truman instead attended a DAR event the very next day, and Powell labeled her the "Last Lady," an epithet that made it into her otherwise laudatory obituary.[102]

POLITICAL DOWNFALL

Powell had a reputation for high living—news articles routinely covered his many homes, sports cars and boats.[103] He enjoyed theater, never missing an opening night if he could help it. His musical tastes were wide ranging; he loved jazz and attended the Salzburg Festival every year. He was frequently described as "arrogant, but with style," a characterization Powell relished. But his larger-than-life style ultimately led to his political downfall. He frequently missed House votes and took numerous trips abroad at public expense.

In 1958, Powell was indicted for income tax evasion. His trial ended with a hung jury. He ran into more legal trouble in 1963, when he lost a slander lawsuit and refused to pay the judgment against him. To avoid being served contempt papers, Powell began avoiding his Harlem district. New York law prohibited serving civil contempt warrants on Sundays, so that was the only day he returned to the City. An investigation into his office finances unearthed multiple improprieties. In January 1967, the House refused to seat him until the Judiciary Committee completed an investigation into his finances. The committee recommended that Powell be censured and fined; however, Powell's enemies instead went in for the kill, setting up a House vote to exclude him from Congress entirely.

As a response, Powell released a record album titled *Keep the Faith, Baby!*, his signature campaign slogan. His constituents did just that, overwhelmingly voting for him in the special election that had been intended to fill his now-vacant seat. That placed Powell in limbo while the courts sorted out his status. (The Supreme Court ultimately found he had been excluded unlawfully.)[104] Powell spent most of that term on the Bahamian island of Bimini. This set the stage for New York State assemblyman Charles Rangel to challenge Powell in the next primary—making Powell's absenteeism a central campaign issue. Rangel defeated Powell by two hundred votes in 1970 and then went on to win the general election. Rangel represented the district until 2017, fending off a 2010 primary challenge by one of Powell's sons.

After his electoral defeat, Powell moved to Bimini, where he continued to live a lifestyle that routinely made headlines. Powell died of cancer on April 4, 1972. In 2005, a monument honoring him was erected in front of the Adam Clayton Powell Jr. State Office Building, at the corner of 125th Street and Adam Clayton Powell Jr. Boulevard. The monument, *Higher Ground* by artist Branly Cadet, depicts Powell striding forward up a steep slope.

Adam Clayton Powell statue. *Courtesy of Jeffrey Bratspies.*

PART II

BRIDGES AND TUNNELS

Chapter 1

GEORGE GOETHALS

THE HERO OF THE CANAL

The Goethals Bridge is named after Major General George Washington Goethals (June 29, 1858–January 22, 1928), who, as chief engineer of the Panama Canal, "performed the greatest feat of engineering the world had known up to his time."[105]

FAMILY LIFE

George Washington Goethals. *Wikimedia Commons.*

Goethals was born in Brooklyn, the second child of Belgian immigrants John Goethals and Marie Baron. They named him after George Washington in honor of their adopted home. According to the *Brooklyn Daily Eagle*, "There was absolutely nothing to indicate that George Goethals, as a baby, was especially precocious."[106]

After passing the City College entrance exam at age fourteen, Goethals spent three years studying medicine while working as a messenger boy to support himself. General Alexander Webb, the Civil War veteran serving as City College president, inspired Goethals toward military service.[107] Then, Congressman Samuel S. Cox nominated Goethals for a vacancy at West Point. At West Point, Goethals studied engineering. He graduated in 1880

FUN FACT President Lincoln was assassinated during Goethals's very first year in school. John Goethals, his older brother, remembered the school, PS 17, draped with black crepe and flags.

at the top of his class, with no demerits—an accomplishment he shared with Robert E. Lee but few others.

In 1884, Goethals married Effie Rodman. Together, they had two sons, George Jr. and Thomas. The elder son, George Jr., followed in his father's footsteps and became a military engineer; Thomas became a physician.

MILITARY CAREER

Upon graduation from West Point, Goethals was commissioned a second lieutenant. He would spend the next thirty-two years—the time between graduation and the Panama Canal—building irrigation works in the West and coastal fortifications in the East.

Goethals's first U.S. Army Corps engineering job was rebuilding a bridge across the Spokane River in the Washington Territories. General William Tecumseh Sherman thought so highly of Goethals that he described him as "the finest young officer on this coast."[108] In 1891, Goethals was promoted to captain and tasked with building a canal along the Tennessee River.[109] Goethals's design set a world record for the highest lock in a canal. It was a design he would re-invoke in the Panama Canal.

The original plans for the Panama Canal had been a sea-level canal along the lines of the Suez Canal. However, Goethals persuaded President Theodore Roosevelt that a lock and high-level lake canal was the better choice.[110] The Senate voted narrowly to approve the plan. In 1907, on the recommendation of Secretary of War William H. Taft, President Roosevelt appointed Goethals chief engineer for the Panama Canal. In doing so, Roosevelt also named Goethals to be a member of the Isthmian Canal Commission with the rank of lieutenant colonel. Soon afterward, Goethals was made the chairman and promoted to the rank of colonel.

Constructing the canal was no mean feat. Goethals took over a demoralized work crew facing seemingly insurmountable obstacles. Goethals's penchant for detail and organization stood him in good stead.

FUN FACT Goethals actually graduated second in his class at West Point, but he was retroactively promoted to first after his classmate Oberlin M. Carter was court-martialed in 1898 for graft and bid fixing during the Savannah Harbor Scandal.

George Washington Goethals with President Taft, inspecting the Panama Canal, December 23, 1910. *Library of Congress.*

Exerting total control over the Canal Zone, Goethals organized all aspects of the project. He managed sanitation, housing and labor, in addition to the design and construction of the canal. His hands-on management style inspired confidence. Under his leadership, the canal administration was as famous for its industrial harmony as for its sound engineering.

After the canal opened, Congress passed an Act of Congress officially thanking Goethals for his service and authorizing President Wilson to promote him to major general.[111] Goethals responded by advocating that Congress also recognize the service of the many civilians who contributed to the construction of the canal.[112]

Goethals's success with the canal made him a national hero. Indeed, even though he never saw active service during a military career that spanned multiple wars, the *New York Times* wrote that "completion of the Panama Canal made General Goethals the most famous engineer who ever wore the uniform of the United States Army, and, next to General Pershing, West Point's best-known graduate since the Civil War."[113]

New York City mayor John Mitchel actively recruited Goethals to become New York City's police commissioner.[114] The key sticking point was Goethals's demand that there be no judicial review when police officers were

FUN FACT In
*Arsenic and Old
Lace*, actor John
Alexander (who
believes he is Teddy
Roosevelt) mistakes
Peter Lorre for
General Goethals
and invites him to
inspect the locks for
the Panama Canal
that Alexander
is digging in the
basement.

fired—a demand that put him in conflict with the police associations. In the end, Goethals did not become police commissioner.[115] Instead, President Wilson appointed General Goethals to be the first civilian governor of the Canal Zone, a post he held from 1914 to 1916.

In 1916, Goethals was appointed state engineer of New Jersey. But two days after he started, the United States declared war against Germany.[116] Within a fortnight, President Wilson had summoned Goethals back to active duty. Secretary of War Newton Baker named Goethals acting quartermaster general of the United States. Reportedly, former president Theodore Roosevelt reacted to the appointment by saying, "I congratulate you, and thrice congratulate the country."[117]

In February 1918, Goethals was made director of purchase, storage and traffic, and he was given the Herculean task of coordinating the entire military supply chain. He was in charge of all purchases for the War Department and was responsible for the domestic transportation and overseas deployment of all troops and supplies.[118] Goethals relied extensively on civilian experts in his quest to centralize and rationalize procurement. Despite his best efforts, Goethals made only marginal progress toward that goal.

Goethals nevertheless received the Distinguished Service Medal in 1918 "for especially meritorious and conspicuous service in reorganizing the Quartermaster Department." Goethals was also decorated by the French government with the Legion of Honor, Order of Commander, for his war service. He was awarded honorary degrees by Chicago, Yale, Harvard, Princeton, University of Pennsylvania and Rutgers and medals from the National Geographic Society and the National Academy of Sciences, among other honors. Every year since 1956, the Society for American Military Engineers has awarded the Goethals Medal to a military engineer who made "eminent and notable contributions" to the field.

FUN FACT Under Goethals's leadership, the Panama Canal was completed ahead of time and under budget. The Panama Canal officially opened on August 15, 1914.* The timing was unfortunate, as just days earlier, Britain and France had declared war on Germany. World War I forced the cancellation of planned festivities, and the first boat to make transit through the canal was a relatively humble cement boat.

* Farnham Bishop, The Builder of the Canal, in The World's Work—a History of Our Times, Vol. 21 at 396 (1912).

GOETHALS BRIDGE

After the war, Goethals became the first consulting engineer to the Port Authority of New York and New Jersey. He died in January 1928 at sixty-nine and was buried at West Point. A few months later, on June 29, 1928, the Goethals Bridge opened on what would have been Goethals's seventieth birthday.

Designed by John Alexander Low Waddell, the Goethals Bridge links Elizabeth, New Jersey, with Staten Island. In 2013, the Port Authority announced a public-private partnership to replace the Waddell bridge with a more modern structure.[119] This new Goethals Bridge was the first bridge built by the Port Authority since it completed the George Washington Bridge in 1927. After construction finished in 2017, the new and improved Goethals Bridge boasted three lanes in each direction, as well as a "shared use" bike and pedestrian path. Unlike the original plans, however, there is no toll for pedestrians or cyclists using the Goethals Bridge. As it is one of the main routes between New Jersey and New York City, roughly 1.3 million vehicles cross the Goethals Bridge each month.

FUN FACT In 1919, the navy commissioned the USS *General G.W. Goethals* as a supply and troop transport ship. During World War II, a steam-powered army troop transport ship was named the USAT *George W. Goethals* in his honor.

Goethals Bridge. *Photo by formulanone from Huntsville, Wikimedia Commons.*

Chapter 2

TADEUSZ KOŚCIUSZKO

THE PUREST SON OF LIBERTY

N ew York City's Kościuszko Bridge was named after General Tadeusz Andrzej Bonawentura Kościuszko (1746–1817).

EARLY LIFE

Born in the Polish-Lithuanian Commonwealth, Kościuszko was the fourth child of Ludwik and Tekla Kościuszko. He was nominated to join the inaugural class of the Royal Knight School, the military academy created by the newly crowned Polish king, Stanislaw II Augustus. Impressed by Kościuszko's talent, King Stanislaw sent Kościuszko to Paris in 1768 for further studies in military engineering. The multifaceted Kościuszko also studied architecture, drawing and painting. While he was in Paris, the Bar Confederation, led in part by Casimir Pulaski (*see entry on Pulaski*), overthrew the king.

One month after the Declaration of Independence was signed, Kościuszko arrived in Philadelphia to participate in the American Revolution. He walked into Benjamin Franklin's print shop and volunteered his engineering

Tadeusz Kościuszko, by Władysław Barwicki. *Wikimedia Commons.*

FUN FACT After the Bar Confederation collapsed, Kościuszko returned to Poland. But he was too poor to purchase an officer's commission and instead took a job as a tutor. He was soon forced to flee with a price on his head after his failed elopement with Ludwika Sosnowski, the daughter of his employer, General Sosnowski. Kościuszko never married.

services to the Continental army. Originally commissioned as colonel of engineers, Kościuszko ultimately mustered out as a brigadier general with a congressional citation for meritorious service.

During his time with the Continental army, Kościuszko designed the fortifications of Philadelphia and West Point (the very plans that were later turned over to the British by Benedict Arnold). Kościuszko's military acumen helped turn the tide of the war. It was Kościuszko's brilliant defense plans (along with the valor of not-yet-traitorous Benedict Arnold) that gave the Continental army its first decisive military victory at the Battle of Saratoga, forcing the surrender of British general John Burgoyne. This victory helped persuade France to enter the conflict as an American ally.

An implacable foe of slavery, Kościuszko's aide de camp was a Black man, Agrippa Hull.[120] Hull was a free New Englander who had enlisted in the Continental army. During the Southern Campaign, Kościuszko's military successes in North and South Carolina relied heavily on information that Hull garnered from his network of Black spies.

In 1784, after mustering out of the American army, Kościuszko returned to his native Poland. There, he again distinguished himself in military service in the cause of freedom, this time fighting Russian occupation. As supreme commander of the Polish National Armed Forces, he led the 1794 Kościuszko Uprising—an attempt to drive Russian forces out of Poland, Lithuania and Belarus.

Kościuszko was a progressive political thinker. As supreme commander, he issued the Proclamation of Polaniec, which partially abolished serfdom in Poland and granted civil liberties to Jews and all peasants. He recruited a Jewish cavalry unit and promised equality for all after the revolution. Unfortunately, despite some initial military successes, the movement that Kościuszko led ultimately

FUN FACT Kościuszko was reportedly moved to tears by the Declaration of Independence and made a point of meeting Thomas Jefferson. The two became close friends and carried on a correspondence for years. Kościuszko's letters to Jefferson focused on the immorality of slavery. Thomas Jefferson characterized Kościuszko as "as pure a son of liberty as I have ever known."

Left: Proclamation of Połaniec.
*Polish Central Archives of Historical
Records, Wikimedia Commons.*

Below: *General Kościuszko Recovering*,
by Benjamin West. *Wikimedia
Commons.*

lost. Kościuszko was wounded seventeen times and captured in the Battle of
Maciejowice. He was imprisoned in St. Petersburg on the orders of Czarina
Catherine the Great.

After Catherine's death, her son Czar Paul I pardoned Kościuszko on
the condition that he not return to Poland. Kościuszko instead went to the

United States to recuperate from his war wounds. In Philadelphia, he was given a hero's welcome—carried through the streets on the shoulders of the crowd while bands played and cannons fired.[121] The home that he lived in at 301 Pine Street in Philadelphia is now a national monument. Reportedly, he met there with Chief Little Turtle (Mihšihkinaahkwa) of the Miami Indians. The two exchanged gifts, with Kościuszko giving Chief Little Turtle the dueling pistols he had received in the Polish military academy with the advice to "shoot dead the first man who comes to subjugate you."[122]

In 1798, Kościuszko hurriedly left the United States for Paris to avoid President John Adams's Alien and Sedition Act. No less a personage than Vice President Thomas Jefferson procured him a fake passport. Before leaving, Kościuszko wrote what became known as his American will—a document dedicating all his American assets to purchase the freedom of enslaved Black men and to pay for their education and provide them with land.[123] He named Thomas Jefferson as the executor of this will. After Kościuszko's death, Jefferson refused to carry out the terms. Litigation over Kościuszko's will lasted for thirty-five years and involved three separate Supreme Court decisions.[124] None of the resources were ever used for manumission or education.[125]

After the French Revolution, "Citizen Kościuszko" was fêted in Paris. Napoleon called him "the Hero of the North." But Citizen Kościuszko never trusted Napoleon, presciently warning fellow revolutionaries about Napoleon's tendency toward dictatorship.[126]

Kościuszko spent the rest of his life in exile, dying in Switzerland in 1817. He was posthumously awarded Poland's highest military honors for his service.

Memorials to Kościuszko exist across the United States and around the world. In 1933, the United States Post Office issued a stamp featuring the statue of Kościuszko that stands in Washington, D.C, near the White House. The highest mountain in Australia is named in his honor.

FUN FACT

Lord Byron posthumously lionized Kościuszko in his epic poem *The Age of Bronze*, writing, "That sound that crashes in the tyrant's ear—Kościuszko!"

KOŚCIUSZKO BRIDGE

The three-lane Kościuszko Bridge opened in 1939, not long after Germany invaded Poland. In naming the bridge after Kościuszko, New York City mayor Fiorello LaGuardia praised Polish liberty, asserting that "in so far as

Kosciuszko Bridge, old and new. *Jim Henderson, Wikimedia Commons.*

the American people and the American government are concerned, the free government of Poland still lives and will continue to live."[127] State Attorney General John Bennett further underscored the political message behind the naming of the Kościuszko Bridge, stating, "When we remember that Poland produced Kościuszko and other great heroes like the great Casimir Pulaski, I am confident that Poland will live again. Any land which breeds such lovers of freedom can never be kept enslaved. The Polish people may be captive, but the flaming spirit of Polish liberty will never be extinguished."[128] During the Second World War, a squadron of exiled Polish pilots flew with the British RAF as the Kościuszko Squadron.

Designed with a steep arch to accommodate high-masted ships, the original Kościuszko Bridge spanned Newtown Creek, connecting the neighborhoods of Maspeth, Queens and Green Point, Brooklyn. It carried nearly 200,000 cars each day. In 2014, the bridge, notorious for gridlock during the morning commute, underwent extensive renovations that expanded the bridge to five lanes and added a bike and pedestrian path. The new Kościuszko Bridge opened in 2017. It is unfortunately just as congested as the old bridge.

Chapter 3

CASIMIR PULASKI

THE NOBLE REVOLUTIONARY

New York City's Pulaski Bridge and New Jersey's Pulaski Skyway were named after General Kazimierz (Casimir) Pulaski (1747–1779).

EARLY LIFE

Casimir Pulaski drawing.
Courtesy of the NYPL.

Kazimierz (Casimir) Michał Władysław Wiktor Pulaski was born on March 4 or 6, 1745, in Warsaw, Poland, to aristocratic parents Joseph Pulaski and Marianna Zielinska. He was one of eight children. As part of an elite family, he grew up in luxury. Along with his father, Joseph, Casimir participated actively in the Bar Confederation, an uprising against Polish king (and Russian puppet) Stanislaw II Augustus. Pulaski was generally considered the most effective military leader in the uprising, though also something of a loose cannon. The Bar Confederation achieved some initial successes, setting up a rival government that won recognition from other European states. However, the Confederation was ultimately defeated, and Pulaski was tried in

Pułaski at Bar, by Korneli Szlegel. *Wikimedia Commons.*

absentia for treason. Condemned to death for his for alleged role in a plot to kidnap the king, Pulaski took refuge in Paris. There he wound up in debtors' prison. But Pulaski still had influential friends who not only paid his debts but also introduced him to the Marquis de Lafayette and Benjamin Franklin, then serving as America's ambassador to France.

REVOLUTIONARY WAR SERVICE

Franklin recommended Pulaski to George Washington as one who was "renowned throughout Europe for the courage and bravery he displayed in defense of his country's freedom."[129] Upon his arrival in the United States in 1777, Pulaski wrote to General Washington, stating, "I came here, where freedom is being defended, to serve it, and to live or die for it."[130]

Widely acclaimed as a war hero both in the United States and in Poland, Pulaski reputedly saved the life of George Washington by rallying disordered Continental army troops during their retreat at the Battle of Brandywine. Commissioned a brigadier general by the Continental Congress, Pulaski was also granted the special title "Commander of the Horse." Pulaski then proceeded to professionalize and organize the Continental army's cavalry, earning him the title the "Father of the American Cavalry." The cavalry unit he formed, the Pulaski Cavalry Legion, fought in Haddonfield, Little Egg Harbor and New Jersey's Osborn Island.

In 1778, Pulaski was stationed in Bethlehem, Pennsylvania, to guard the county's Moravian inhabitants from British attack. Local women made him a cavalry banner, which Pulaski brought to the southern theater of war the following year. Henry Wadsworth Longfellow memorialized the story of Pulaski's banner in his 1840 poem "Hymn of the Moravian Nuns of Bethlehem at the Consecration of Pulaski's Banner."[131]

In February 1779, Pulaski's cavalry, carrying the Bethlehem banner, helped defend Charleston, South Carolina, from British attack. Pulaski was put in command of the combined American and French cavalry. On the morning of October 9, 1779, Pulaski was mortally wounded during the Siege of Savannah. He was taken aboard the American ship USS *Wasp*, where he died on October 11, 1779, at the ripe old age of thirty-two. There were conflicting accounts of what happened to his body. He was either buried at sea, buried in South Carolina or buried at Greenwich Plantation in Georgia. In an extravagant 1824 ceremony that included the Marquis de Lafayette, the City of Savannah unveiled a memorial commemorating both Pulaski and his Revolutionary War contemporary Nathanael Greene. Nearly three

---

FUN FACT In the early years of the twenty-first century, Pulaski's body was exhumed. Forensic examination resulted in a startling discovery—the bones, which showed evidence of the wounds Pulaski was known to suffer, had a characteristically female pelvis.* Many other characteristics of the bones suggest that Pulaski was intersex—a general term that applies to those born with "a reproductive or sexual anatomy that doesn't seem to fit the typical definitions of female or male."† Other circumstances of Pulaski's life—particularly Pulaski's slight, slender stature; the fact that he never married and had no children; and his reputation for extreme privacy even on the battlefield—offered some contemporaneous support. In 2015, anthropology professor Virginia Hutton Estabrook conclusively matched mitochondrial DNA from these remains with one of Pulaski's known relatives (who died in 1800). Pulaski presented as male throughout his life and may have been unaware of this condition.

---

* Jack Pinkowski, Mysteries Surrounding Casimir Pulaski, White Eagle (Apr. 18, 2008).
† Brigit Katz, Was the Revolutionary War Hero Casimir Pulaski Intersex? Smithsonian (Apr. 9, 2019).

decades later, Savannah erected a fifty-foot obelisk honoring Pulaski alone. At that time, Pulaski's putative grave at Greenwich Plantation was exhumed, and the bones were reinterred under the monument. It took until 2015 to confirm that these bones were in fact Pulaski's.

In Pulaski's Honor

Across the United States, numerous places and events are named in Pulaski's honor, including counties in Georgia, Kentucky, Illinois, Arkansas and Virginia. There is also Fort Pulaski in Georgia, the submarine USS *Pulaski* and various commemorative statues in Rhode Island, Connecticut, Massachusetts, Washington, D.C., and Maryland, in addition to the monument in Savannah. In 1867, Congress appropriated $1,000 for a bust of Pulaski, which stands alongside Kościuszko in the U.S. Senate vestibule. In 1929, Congress declared October 11 (the date of his death) to be Casimir Pulaski Day, and in 2009, President Obama signed a Joint Resolution of Congress that posthumously awarded Pulaski honorary American citizenship.

Pulaski Bridge sign. *Photo by Rebecca Bratspies.*

In 1931, Pulaski was commemorated on a two-cent stamp. In Illinois, the first Monday in March is celebrated as Casimir Pulaski Day. Sufjan Stevens wrote the song "Casimir Pulaski Day," which was recorded on his album *Illinoise*.

The Pulaski Bridge crosses Newtown Creek and connects the Queens neighborhood of Long Island City with the Brooklyn neighborhood of Greenpoint. A drawbridge, the Pulaski Bridge is the unofficial halfway point in the annual New York City Marathon. Roughly 37,000 vehicles cross the Pulaski Bridge each day. In 2016, New York City added dedicated bike lanes to the bridge, and thousands of cyclists commute across it each day.

The Pulaski Skyway

The most notable infrastructure named for Casimir Pulaski is the Pulaski Skyway, a 3.5-mile viaduct that crosses the New Jersey Meadowlands and the Hackensack and Passaic Rivers. Part of America's first superhighway, the Pulaski Skyway was a remarkable feat of engineering. Funded, planned and designed by the New Jersey State Highway Commission, it cost $20 million to build ($410 million in 2020 dollars), making it the most expensive bridge of its era.[132] The Skyway was intended to solve two interrelated traffic problems: the illogical and diffuse structure of the Port of New York and New Jersey (*see entry on Outerbridge*) and the traffic jams that gridlocked the region.

Between 1900 and 1920, New York City was the busiest port in the country, handling one-fifth of the nation's foreign commerce. Yet many of the railroads terminated in Jersey City. Connecting rail and marine transit meant putting train cars on barges and floating them across the Hudson River. Sheer complexity made this system chaotic at the best of times, and World War I broke it entirely. Labor shortages coupled with a particularly harsh winter left goods languishing on boxcars in Jersey City. New York became a transportation bottleneck, which, in turn, created food and fuel shortages all along the East Coast. The newly created Port Authority of New York and New Jersey sought to solve this problem by building the Holland Tunnel (*see entry on Holland*). Unfortunately, the solution in its turn produced a new set of problems—most notably massive traffic jams at the tunnels' endpoints.

New Jersey's solution to gridlock was the Pulaski Skyway—a limited-access superhighway that could channel traffic from the Holland Tunnel through the region without burdening local streets. Designed by Danish engineer Sigvald Johannesson and constructed between 1923 and 1932, the yet-to-be-named roadway opened on Thanksgiving Day 1932. The following May, the New Jersey legislature voted to name the road the General Casimir Pulaski Memorial Skyway.

FUN FACT Pulaski is one of only eight people to be awarded honorary United States citizenship. The others are Winston Churchill, Mother Teresa, William and Hannah Penn, Raoul Wallenberg, the Marquis de Lafayette and the Viscount of Galveston.

The Pulaski Skyway was designed to accommodate warships traveling up the rivers to the Port of New York. With that in mind, the Skyway's cantilevered trusses stand on concrete columns that tower up to 135 feet above high tide levels. The Pulaski Skyway

Pulaski Skyway. *Library of Congress.*

originally had two 10-foot-wide travel lanes in each direction, with a breakdown lane in the center. There were no shoulders and no provisions for pedestrian traffic. Unfortunately, this design encouraged motorists to use the breakdown lane as a passing lane, leading to a high number of head-on collisions. To resolve the situation, road designers replaced the center breakdown lane with a concrete median that kept the northbound and southbound traffic separated, thereby preventing cross-over collisions. This median became known as a "Jersey barrier."

When the Pulaski Skyway opened, the American Institute of Steel Construction named it the "Most Beautiful Steel Structure" among long-span bridges.[133] It is registered on the New Jersey and National Registers of Historic Places. It was featured in the opening of *The Sopranos*, and in Orson Welles's radio drama *War of the Worlds*, the Pulaski Skyway let invading Martians into New York City.

Roughly 86,000 cars use the Pulaski Skyway each day.

Chapter 4

EUGENIUS OUTERBRIDGE

THE BUSINESS MOGUL

The Outerbridge Crossing was named after Eugenius Harvey Outerbridge (March 8, 1860–November 10, 1932), a businessman who served as the first chairman of the Port Authority, then called the Port of New York Authority.

FAMILY LIFE

Eugenius Harvey Outerbridge. *Library of Congress.*

Eugenius Outerbridge was born in Philadelphia to prominent Bermudian parents Alexander Ewing Outerbridge and Laura Katherine Harvey. He was one of ten children. One of his brothers, Sir Joseph Outerbridge, was knighted by King George in 1913, and his sister Mary is famous for bringing tennis to the United States.

Outerbridge spent much of his career in his family import-export business. In 1909, he brought the then-secret process for manufacturing fiberboard from recycled newspapers to the United States. He built a factory in Trenton, New Jersey, and formed the Agasote Millboard Company to produce fiberboard panels for use in railroad cars. Within a few years, the company also began producing automobile tops. During World War I, the company produced a new kind of panel—lightweight, weather-resistant fiberboard called Homasote. This new product was used to build field hospitals and military housing. After the war, Outerbridge changed the company's name to Homasote to reflect this new focus. Today, the Homasote Company is the United States' oldest manufacturer of green building products from recycled materials.

PORT AUTHORITY

Because his business relied heavily on shipping, Outerbridge became a proponent of plans to alleviate the terrible congestion in the Port of New York. As president of New York's chamber of commerce from 1916 to 1918, Outerbridge championed the proposal that New York and New Jersey form a bistate Port Authority.

It was a hard sell. In 1916, New York and New Jersey were engaged in a monumental fight over shipping rates charged by the railroads operating in the port. New Jersey had taken the dispute to the Interstate Commerce Commission in a case that was viewed as "the culmination of two and a half centuries of bickering over an imaginary line dividing the harbor against itself."[134] The Interstate Commerce Commission concluded that "[h]istorically, geographically, and commercially New York and the industrial district in the northern part of the state of New Jersey constitute a single community" and ordered that the two states work together to resolve their issues.[135] However, the forces arrayed against such state-to-state cooperation were significant. The Tammany Hall political machine opposed the formation of the Port Authority, and New York City mayor John Francis Hylan did all he could to thwart its formation.[136] The twelve private railroads operating in the port also fought Outerbridge's attempts at coordination.

During World War I, the port of New York and New Jersey became the major embarkation point for the American Expeditionary Forces and supplies heading toward Europe. Problems with congestion at the port suddenly became a national priority. In 1918, New York governor Al Smith named Outerbridge to the New York, New Jersey Port and Harbor Development Commission. The commission recommended that the two states create a single Port Authority with

FUN FACT The Outerbridge Crossing was named a "crossing" to avoid calling it the Outerbridge Bridge.*

---

* New York Bridge Is Named for Family Named for Bridge, N.Y. Times (Apr. 25, 1926).

jurisdiction over the entire port district.[137] Acting on this guidance, New York and New Jersey created the Port of New York Authority on April 30, 1921. The Port Authority has the distinction of being the first interstate agency created under the clause in Article 1, Section 10 of the United States Constitution, which requires congressional approval for compacts between states. By statute, Outerbridge became one of the inaugural commissioners of the Port Authority.[138]

FUN FACT Outerbridge's main claim to fame may be his work with the Port Authority, but he was considered an expert on transportation more generally, testifying before Congress on tariff plans for the Panama Canal and against the proposal for dredging a channel in the St. Lawrence Seaway.

During a special meeting of the New York Chamber of Commerce, Outerbridge had the honor of being the first signatory to the original compact creating the Port Authority.[139] New Jersey governor Edwards, who had vetoed the compact only to have his veto overturned by the New Jersey legislature, boycotted the proceedings. New York City mayor Hylan similarly refused to take part in the ceremony, and none of New York City's borough presidents attended. The Port Authority's first order of business was to elect Outerbridge to be chairman. In that capacity, he created a comprehensive plan for the development of the port. General George Goethals (*see entry on Goethals*) was named the authority's first consulting engineer.[140]

Describing the Port Authority as "the guardian of the port," Outerbridge advocated for the Port Authority's independence—highlighting its ability to work across state lines and to issue its own bonds as key to its success.[141] Under Outerbridge's leadership, the Port Authority staked out a position that private actors should not have control over the key infrastructure of the port.[142] This part of the comprehensive plan immediately ran into opposition from the railroads, which had little interest in coordinating with one another or reducing fees. It took the intervention of the Interstate Commerce Commission to force the railroads to cooperate with the Port Authority.[143] In advancing the Port Authority's interests, Outerbridge also frequently butted heads with New York City mayor Hylan, who had resisted the formation of the Port Authority every step of the way.[144] New York City owned half the waterfront in the entire port district and was resistant to anything that stripped away local development powers. Mayor Hylan characterized the port plan as "simply another method of grabbing the Port of New York" from its citizens. In turn, Outerbridge was quoted as advising Mayor Hylan to "refrain from issuing statements before he has discovered what the facts are."[145]

While serving as commissioner of the Port Authority, Outerbridge simultaneously held the post of chair of the New York State Fuel Commission. In that capacity, Outerbridge worked closely with Secretary of Commerce Herbert Hoover to develop a coal rationing plan in response to the 1919–21 coal worker strikes.[146] The plan involved raising an unlimited sum of money from New York bankers and financiers to pay for coal shipments. During the height of his influence, Outerbridge was such a pivotal public figure that it was news if he was ill with a cold.[147]

As Port Authority commissioner, Outerbridge oversaw the construction of the George Washington Bridge, the Bayonne Bridge, the Goethals Bridge and the bridge that ultimately bore his name—the Outerbridge Crossing. Upon his retirement, the *New York Times* lauded Outerbridge as "a useful citizen," noting that "in the midst of the confusing charges of selfish and even venal use of public office, it is a relief to turn to the record of Mr. E.H. Outerbridge."[148]

In Outerbridge's time, the Port Authority was considered "perhaps the most efficiently run public works agency in the world"[149] because of its "freedom from niches filled by political patronage."[150] By 2014, however, that description seemed laughably naive. That was the year New Jersey governor Chris Christie's Port Authority allies engineered the closure of George Washington Bridge access lanes to score political points. Email messages announcing, "Time for some traffic problems in Ft. Lee," made it clear that the closures were retaliation against Fort Lee's mayor for his refusal to endorse Christie's reelection campaign.[151] The Supreme Court described the ensuing "BridgeGate" scandal as showing "wrongdoing—deception, corruption, abuse of power."[152]

FUN FACT Outerbridge was given a special badge that allowed him to cross all the Port Authority's bridges free of charge. However, Outerbridge almost always forgot to bring the badge and had to pay the toll instead.*

---

* Alfonso A. Narvaez, An Outerbridge Crosses His Bridge, Now 50, Free, N.Y. Times (Jun. 21, 1978).

OUTERBRIDGE CROSSING

The Outerbridge Crossing was designed by John Alexander Low Waddell. The 750-foot cantilevered structure cost $9.6 million to build. The outermost bridge in the New York/New Jersey port district, the Outerbridge Crossing spans the Arthur Kill to connect the Tottenville section of Staten Island with

Outerbridge Crossing. *Library of Congress.*

Perth Amboy, New Jersey. Like the Pulaski Skyway (*see entry on Pulaski*), it was designed with 143-foot clearance to allow passage of warships.

The Outerbridge Crossing and the Goethals Bridge (*see entry on Goethals*) opened on June 29, 1928. Both bridges were completed ahead of schedule and under budget.[153] They were Port Authority's first bistate development project, with the costs shared equally by New York and New Jersey. The two state legislatures appropriated $2 million for the two bridges and authorized a $14 million bond issue to cover the rest. The bonds would be paid back from proceeds of the tolls. By the end of 1929, the Port Authority reported that more than 812,705 vehicles had crossed the Outerbridge Crossing, and 970,782 had crossed the Goethals. While tolls collected at the Goethals Bridge had generated nearly a $100,000 surplus over operating expenses, the Outerbridge Crossing "had not fulfilled expectations" and was operating at a deficit.[154] For comparison, the Holland Tunnel served 12 million vehicles over the same period.[155]

In 1928, tolls on the Outerbridge Crossing were $0.10 for pedestrians, $0.25 for bicycles and motorcycles, $0.50 for passenger cars, $0.50 to $1.00 for trucks and $1.00 to $1.50 for buses.[156] Today, the Outerbridge Crossing has cashless tolling, and tolls are only collected on traffic entering New York. The toll is $16.00 for cars and motorcycles, $27.00 for buses, and truck tolls range from $44.00 to $136.00, depending on size. Pedestrians and bicycles are not allowed. More than 14 million vehicles use the Outerbridge Crossing each year, with more than 90 percent paying through E-ZPass.[157]

Chapter 5

THE MACOMBS

SPECULATORS (ALEXANDER), SOLDIERS (GENERAL ALEXANDER JR.) AND GRIFTERS (ROBERT)

Macomb's Dam Bridge and Macomb's Dam Park are named after land speculator Alexander Macomb and his sons General Alexander Macomb Jr. and Robert Macomb.

ALEXANDER MACOMB, THE LAND SPECULATOR

Alexander Macomb (July 27, 1748–January 19, 1831) was born in Ireland. As a young child, he immigrated with his parents and siblings to Albany, New York. As young men, Alexander and his brother William moved west to the Fort Detroit area, where they traded with the British, the French and the Potawatomi. In 1773, Alexander Macomb married Mary Catherine Navarre, daughter of a prominent French official. Together, they had eight children.

Alexander and William were remarkably successful fur traders, in part because of their willingness to illegally exchange rum for furs. They parlayed their trading riches into land speculation. In 1776, Alexander and William purchased large swaths of land in the Detroit area from the Potawatomi, including what is now Grosse Ile and Belle Isle. As the Revolutionary War spread to the frontier, Alexander and William became wartime profiteers, amassing wealth by providing the British with scarce merchandise and military supplies. After the war ended, the brothers parted company, with Alexander moving to New York City while William remained in Detroit (which was still under British rule). To this day, an entire county in Michigan bears the name Macomb. William later served as a judge before being elected to the first Parliament of Upper Canada. At his death in 1796, William was the largest slaveholder in Michigan, having enslaved twenty-six Black Americans.

In 1785, Alexander and Mary Catherine moved their family to New York City. Alexander quickly became a successful land speculator. He made a fortune buying and selling thousands of acres in New York, as well as Ohio, North Carolina, Georgia and Kentucky.

Alexander Macomb, by Theodore Parsons Hall. *Wikimedia Commons.*

Despite having sided with the British during the war, the wealthy Macombs were readily accepted into New York City's nouveau riche society. They built a massive four-story house on Broadway near Trinity Church and had more than twenty servants attending to their needs. Alexander was the third-largest slaveholder in the city, having enslaved twelve African Americans.

Mary Catherine died in 1789. At that point, Alexander rented out the elaborate Broadway house, first to the French ambassador and then to President Washington, who used it as his official presidential residence. The next year, Alexander remarried, to Jane Marshall Rucker, the widow of one of his business partners. Together, they had seven children.

However, Alexander's fortunes were about to change dramatically for the worse.

MACOMB'S PURCHASE (AND COLLAPSE)

In 1792, Alexander bought more than 3.5 million acres of "waste and unappropriated land" from the State of New York at about one shilling (one eighth of a dollar) an acre. Known as Macomb's Purchase, this transaction involved roughly 12 percent of the land in the state. It included the Adirondacks (which for many years were known as "Macomb's Mountains"),[158] as well as all the Thousand Islands on St. Lawrence River. It was the single biggest land sale in New York. All this land had been traditional territory of the Seven Tribes (Iroquois) that was confiscated after they sided with the British during the Revolutionary War.[159]

FUN FACT To this day, all the land deeds in New York's present-day Lewis, Jefferson, St. Lawrence and Franklin Counties, as well as in portions of Herkimer and Oswego Counties, trace their origins back to Macomb's Purchase.

The sale of so much state land for such a low price outraged the public and sparked an exhaustive legislative investigation. New York senator Aaron Burr and governor DeWitt Clinton were accused of corruption and collusion in the transaction. There were even allegations that Governor Clinton was conspiring with the Canadian governor to annex the St. Lawrence to Canada. These charges ultimately proved to be baseless.

Although it was officially known as Macomb's Purchase, Alexander worked with two partners—fellow Friendly Sons of St. Patrick's members William Constable and Daniel McCormick. Their purchase was wholly speculative. The partners paid no money up front, promising installment payments spread out over the next six years as they sold the land to settlers and developers.[160] However, at the same time, Alexander was also scheming with William Duer to monopolize the United States debt market. Their "mad speculation" created an immense financial bubble and sparked the Panic of 1792.[161] Both Duer and Alexander wound up in debtors' prison, and Alexander's share of the Macomb's Purchase was broken up and sold to pay his debts.

With assistance from friends, Alexander freed himself from debtors' prison and salvaged some of his fortune. In 1798, he and Jane purchased one hundred acres in the Bronx, where they built a large stone mansion. Two years later, Alexander received a "water grant" from the City of New York. In exchange for an annual $12.50 payment, he obtained the right to use the water in Spuyten Duyvil Creek near the Harlem bridge.[162] Alexander built a large gristmill across the entire creek, using the ebb and flow of the tidal creek to turn the mill. This mill made it impossible for boats to navigate the

FUN FACT In a letter to his partner William Constable, who incidentally wound up with most of the land, Alexander blamed Duer, lamenting, "I curse myself for my credulity....What a pleasant situation I was in....Now see the contrast—my credit gone...a large family to support...and myself going to prison—what a sad reverse, and all this in less than three months."[*]

Alexander's other purchasing partner, Daniel McCormick, was instrumental in thwarting Macomb's monopoly scheme. McCormick is generally memorialized as "the last man in New York to wear knee breeches and silver-buckled shoes."[†]

[*] David B. Dills, Portrait of an Opportunist: The Life of Alexander Macomb, Watertown Daily Times (Sept. 1990).
[†] Id.

creek, even though the express terms of his water grant required Alexander to leave a fifteen-foot passage clear for navigation.

Alexander and his wife, Jane, mortgaged this property as security for a loan of $10,000. When they were unable to pay back the loan, the mill was sold in a foreclosure auction in 1810.[163] Alexander's youngest son, Robert, purchased the mill at the auction.

That same year, more than 100,000 acres of Alexander's remaining landholdings were sold at auction, including Bear Mountain and other lands near New York City.[164] Alexander moved to Washington, D.C., to live with his son General Alexander Macomb Jr. and died in 1831 in Georgetown, Virginia.

GENERAL ALEXANDER MACOMB JR., THE HERO OF PLATTSBURGH (APRIL 3, 1782–JUNE 25, 1841)

Alexander Macomb Jr. had an illustrious military career. In 1798, at the age of sixteen, Alexander Jr. was invited to join the New York Rangers—an elite local militia. The next year, at the recommendation of Alexander Hamilton, who characterized him as "young, active, and ambitious,"[165] Alexander Jr.

General Alexander Macomb Jr., engraving by James Longacre after a painting by Thomas Sully. *National Gallery of Art.*

was commissioned as a cornet of Light Dragoons and rapidly promoted to second lieutenant. He served as secretary to the commission charged with negotiating with the Muscogee (Creek) and the Cherokee on behalf of the United States.[166] In that capacity, he witnessed the 1802 land cessation treaties.

Just a few years later, Alexander Jr. became one of the first officers trained at West Point in the newly created U.S. Army Corps of Engineers. After graduating, Alexander Jr. was appointed a judge advocate and wrote *The Practice of Courts Martial*, the first treatise on American courts-martial and military law.[167]

Alexander Jr. married Harriet Balch Wilson in 1826. They had no children.

War of 1812

Macomb Congressional Medal of Honor, engraved by Moritz Fuerst. *Donated to Wikimedia Commons by the Metropolitan Museum of Art.*

In 1812, Alexander Jr. was promoted to colonel and given command of an artillery regiment. Two years later, having been promoted to brigadier general, Alexander Jr. mustered a small band of regular and volunteer troops to defeat a much larger British-Canadian invasion force at Plattsburgh, New York. Knowing he and his troops would be greatly outnumbered, Alexander Jr. used a strategy he called abattis—building a maze of fake, narrow roads that led the British into dead-end traps where they were vulnerable to ambush. This victory paved the way for the Treaty of Ghent, which ended the war.

Hailed as the "Hero of Plattsburgh," Alexander Jr. received a Congressional Medal of Honor and an official proclamation extending the "Thanks of Congress" for his stunning victory.[168] President James Madison brevetted him to the rank of major general. In 1828, Alexander Jr. got into a very public quarrel with the U.S. Army's two other generals—Generals Winfield Scott and Edmund P. Gaines—over who outranked whom. General Scott publicly called on President John Quincy Adams to arrest and court-martial Alexander Jr.[169] President Adams responded, but not as Scott had hoped. Instead, President Adams appointed Alexander Jr. the commanding general

NOT-SO-FUN FACT General Scott presided over Cherokee removal, ordering his soldiers to evict Cherokee from their homes at bayonet point. In 1836, Generals Scott and Gaines were both relieved of commands and ordered to appear before a military tribunal inquiring into their conduct during the Second Seminole War. This conflict was sparked by the United States' attempt to evict Seminole and Creek Indians from their lands in the wake of the Supreme Court decision in *Cherokee Nation v. Georgia*. Alexander Jr. presided over this inquiry. Both Gaines and Scott tried to disqualify Alexander Jr. on the grounds that he held a grudge about their earlier attempt to court-martial him and would not be impartial. Nevertheless, the inquiry ultimately rejected allegations of misconduct against both officers.* Scott went on to run for president as a the last-ever Whig nominee. Scott's antislavery reputation contributed to his overwhelming loss to Franklin Pierce.

---

* Proceedings of the Military Court of Inquiry in the Case of Major General Scott and Major General Gaines, printed in pursuance of a resolution of the Senate of March 3, 1837.

of the United States Army, a post he held until his death. Alexander Jr. later petitioned Congress to retroactively increase his pay because Gaines and Scott had been paid more than him.[170]

General Alexander Macomb Jr. died of apoplexy on June 25, 1841.[171] A statue honoring him stands in downtown Detroit.

ROBERT MACOMB: THE GRIFTER
(DECEMBER 28, 1783–FEBRUARY 4, 1832)

Robert Macomb, painting by Edward Greene Malbone. *Donated to Wikimedia Commons by the Metropolitan Museum of Art.*

Alexander Macomb's youngest child with his first wife, Mary Catherine, was Robert Macomb. After graduating from Columbia College in 1802, Robert became a lawyer and served as clerk of the New York Court of General Sessions. In 1806, Robert married Mary Cornell Pell. Mary's wealth and her ties to both the Cornell and Pell families ensured that the wedding was a society affair. The pair married at Trinity Church under the auspices of Reverend Benjamin Moore. Together, they had one daughter, Julia.

SCANDAL

During the War of 1812, Robert left the court to join the military. He held the rank of lieutenant colonel in the U.S. Army, serving as an aide to Governor Tompkins of New York. After the war, Robert returned to his post as clerk of court, where he rapidly ran into controversy. In 1817, William Coleman (editor of the *Evening Post* before William Cullen Bryant—*see entry on Bryant*) accused Robert of malfeasance, alleging that Robert was "prostituting" his office as clerk of court "to the vilest, meanest, most mercenary and even dishonest purposes."[172] Specifically, Coleman alleged that Robert had been selling pardons to convicted criminals and had preyed on the poor by pocketing fines and bail money paid into the court.[173] Robert brought a libel action against Coleman and lost spectacularly— Coleman easily persuading a jury in his favor on the ground that that truth was an absolute defense to libel.[174] Robert was forced to step down as a clerk of the court.[175]

Macomb's Dam(n) Bridge

In 1813, Robert successfully petitioned the New York legislature for permission to build a dam across the Harlem River at 155th Street (to furnish power for the mill his father had built and lost).[176] The authorizing legislation explicitly required that Robert build a lock and provide a lockkeeper to maintain passage for boats and vessels navigating up and down the river. There was a five-dollar statutory penalty (plus litigation expenses) for every instance of obstruction or delay in the passage of such boats. However, Robert did not build the required lock. As a result, most boats could only pass the dam at low tide, and vessels with masts could not get through at all.

This legislation also required that Robert receive permission from the City of New York before building his dam. In 1816, in exchange for his promise to pay an annual rent of $12.50 (the same as his father before him), the City of New York granted Robert permission to build the dam.[177] However, the City rejected Robert's petition to build a toll bridge on top of his dam. Robert built his bridge anyway and then proceeded to charge a toll to cross it.

Unfortunately, Robert's foray into milling was no more successful than his father's had been. By 1817, Robert was insolvent. His creditors were jostling for position as they foreclosed on the mortgages secured by the dam and the mill.[178] The property, along with the water grant, was once again sold via sheriff sale, this time to Duncan Campbell, a family connection of Robert's wife, Mary.

FUN FACT Until 1848, New York's coverture law barred married women from directly owning any property. Mary, who had come to her marriage a wealthy woman, owned much of the land surrounding the mill. After she married Robert, Mary's land was held in trust, with Columbia professor James Renwick acting as trustee.*

Campbell and Mary (through Renwick) cooked up a scheme to build a second dam and to convert Macomb's dam and Mary's land into an industrial hub along the lines of Paterson. To this end, they formed the New York Hydraulic Company and solicited a testimonial from General Alexander Jr. to add credibility to the plan and vouch for its technical feasibility.

---

* Stammer v. Macomb, 2 Wend. 454 (1829).

Confrontation at Macomb's Dam(n) Bridge

Robert's activities and Mary's development plans infuriated Lewis Morris, whose Haerlem Bridge Company had previously been granted the exclusive right to build bridges across the Harlem River.[179] Indeed, Robert's 1813 grant from the New York legislature had carefully stated that "nothing in this Act shall be construed to affect, injure, or impair any rights, property or privilege which may now be vested by law...the Haerlem Bridge company."

Moreover, the lack of a lock or passage through Macomb's dam was wreaking havoc with river traffic. Leading Westchester citizens organized to voice their outrage. In September 1839, they decided to take matters into their own hands. To that end, Morris and other Westchester leaders showed up at Macomb's dam aboard the *Superior*, a schooner laden with coal. They demanded passage through the (nonexistent) lock. Since passage was obviously impossible, Morris and his allies proceeded to dismantle part of the dam to create a passageway for their vessel.[180]

Campbell and Mary tried to have Morris indicted for criminal trespass, but Recorder Riker (*see entry on Riker*) refused to allow a grand jury to consider the matter, finding that Morris had the right to demand passage. They then tried to sue Morris for damaging the dam. They lost. The jury found the dam to be a public nuisance. Because the dam owners had no right to obstruct navigation on the Harlem River, the court found that Morris had been entitled to remove "as much of the dam as was necessary to allow safe and convenient passage for all vessels at any tide."[181]

In 1854, the City of New York repossessed Macomb's dam, alleging that the $12.50 annual rent had not been paid since 1816.[182] In 1858, the New

FUN FACT Edward Hopper's 1935 painting memorializing Macomb's Dam Bridge hangs in the Brooklyn Museum.

Macomb's Dam Bridge, painting by Edward Hopper. *Wikimedia Commons.*

York legislature finally directed New York City and Westchester County to remove the dam and build a new toll-free bridge.[183] To facilitate navigation, this bridge was built as a swing bridge. The current Macomb's Dam Bridge, a massive swinging steel span designed by engineer Alfred P. Boller, opened in 1896. At the time, it was the world's heaviest movable object. Macomb's Dam Bridge was landmarked in 1992.

MACOMB'S DAM PARK

The 1813 grant to Robert also included a triangular piece of land near the dam. In the late 1890s, the City used eminent domain to acquire this land and created Macomb's Dam Park. In 1918, a proposed street widening threatened the park. However, in light of popular opposition, the parks commissioner assured concerned residents that "Macomb's Dam Park will not be molested."[184]

In 2006, New York City reached a land-swap deal with the Yankees to allow construction of a new baseball stadium on the Macomb's Dam Park site. In exchange, the Yankees rebuilt Macomb's Dam Park on the old stadium site. The new Macomb's Dam Park opened in 2010.

FUN FACT In 1933, New York City held a "healthiest baby" competition in Macomb's Dam Park. The prize-winning babies were displayed in the arms of police officers and in a parade led by the police band.*

* 300 Babies in Show at Macombs Park, N.Y. Times (Oct. 8, 1933).

Chapter 6

CLIFFORD HOLLAND

THE HEAD MOLE

The Holland Tunnel was named for Clifford Milburn Holland (March 13, 1883–October 7, 1924), the chief engineer of the project.

FAMILY LIFE

Clifford Holland was born in Somerset, Massachusetts, to Edward John Holland and Lydia Frances Hood. A sickly child, Holland suffered from a weak heart and was limited in his activities. Perhaps because of these limits, Holland was a dedicated and ambitious student. In 1906, he received a BS in civil engineering from Harvard University (having received a BA the year before).

Armed with these degrees, Holland immediately headed to New York City. Indeed, on the very day he graduated from Harvard, Holland took up a post as an assistant engineer for the City.[185] In that role, Hudson worked on the first subway tunnel going under the East River—connecting the Battery in Manhattan with Joralemon Street in Brooklyn. The Joralemon tunnel opened in 1908. That same year, Holland married Anna Coolidge Davenport (1885–1973), with whom he had four daughters.

Clifford Holland. *Library of Congress.*

DIGGING TUNNELS

A truly gifted engineer, Holland rapidly advanced in his career. By 1915, he was already the engineer-in-charge for four subway tunnel projects under the East River. By the time those projects were completed, Holland had a well-deserved reputation as the nation's leading tunnel expert.

While Holland was busy designing subway tunnels, New York was falling in love with the automobile. Henry Ford and his competitors were mass-producing cars by the thousands. The island of Manhattan was woefully unprepared for the traffic problems associated with all those vehicles. At the time, the only way across the Hudson River was via an eighteen-minute ferry ride crammed with both horse-drawn and motorized traffic. More than thirty-one thousand vehicles made the watery trek each day. The "intolerable" congestion[186] meant long wait times to board the ferries, and the traffic headaches spilled out from the docks to affect everyone traveling along the river. Moreover, the ferries were at the mercy of fog and ice—indeed, in December 1917, a spate of bad weather shut down all traffic, creating a "coal famine" that nearly brought New York City to its knees.[187]

A TUNNEL UNDER THE HUDSON

The states of New York and New Jersey recognized that they had a real problem. Together, they appointed a joint commission tasked with resolving congestion. Originally, the plan was to build a bridge, but to avoid interfering with shipping, such a bridge would need a minimum of two hundred feet clearance. The commission concluded that a tunnel would be more economically and technically feasible. Thus, the Hudson River Vehicular Tunnel was born. Proponents claimed that the tunnel would not only end congestion but also "make motor car traffic between New York and Jersey City a matter of pleasure."[188]

Eleven different tunnel plans were submitted to the Port Authority, including one by General George W. Goethals (*see entry on Goethals*), who had

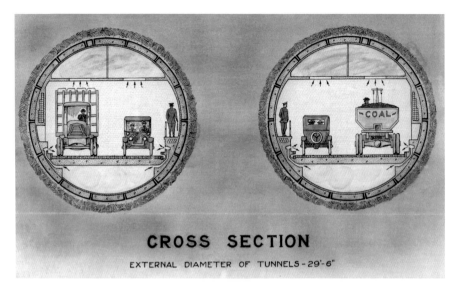

CROSS SECTION

EXTERNAL DIAMETER OF TUNNELS - 29'-6"

Hudson River Vehicular Tunnel. *New York Public Library Digital Collections.*

spent years advocating for such a tunnel. However, Holland's plan, which proposed two cast-iron tunnel tubes, each containing two lanes of traffic, was selected over Goethals's proposal for a single concrete-block tube.[189] Thus, in 1919, Holland was unanimously named chief engineer on the project. He was thirty-six years old.

The construction plan called for the two states to split the $48.4 million cost of the tunnel. New York's assembly passed their bill unanimously.[190] But New Jersey governor Edwards vetoed the funding bill that would have provided New Jersey's share of the construction costs. In May 1920, the New Jersey legislature overrode the veto, thereby allowing work to start. Work began on the New York side after a groundbreaking ceremony on October 12, 1920, at the foot of Canal Street in Manhattan. Reportedly, work did not begin on the New Jersey side until Holland and some engineers snuck over in the middle of the night and personally began digging.[191]

FUN FACT John Alexander Low Waddell, designer of the Goethals Bridge and the Outerbridge Crossing, argued against automobile tunnels under the Hudson in favor of bridges, claiming, *inter alia,* that "the general public almost to a man (and certainly to a woman) would always greatly prefer driving over a structure that provides good air and light, and usually a fine view of the harbor and the surrounding country in comparison with traversing a long, cramped and dingy tube."*

* J.A.L. Waddell, Bridge versus Tunnel for the Proposed Hudson River Crossing at New York City, American Society for Engineers, Paper No. 1477 (1921).

FUN FACT During the construction of what would become the Holland Tunnel, Holland spent so much time at the construction site that newspaper reporters began calling him the "Head Mole."

Tunnel construction workers, so-called sand hogs, spent the next year digging through mud and blasting through rock. The work was hard and dangerous. Over the course of construction, hundreds of sand hogs got "the bends" from the sudden changes of air pressure as workers descended into and rose out of the tunnels. Thirteen workers died on the job.

Once described as the "Eighth Wonder of the World" and "engineering perfection,"[192] the Holland Tunnel is truly an engineering masterpiece. Made up of twin tubes that were 29.5 feet in diameter, the tunnel stretches 8,557 feet long, more than 5,200 of which are under the Hudson River.[193] At its deepest point, the tunnel is 93.5 feet below the surface. Building it required excavating 500,000 cubic yards of soil and rock and used 115,000 tons of cast iron and 13,000 cubic yards of concrete.[194] The tunnel was designed to accommodate 3,800 vehicles an hour, roughly 15 million per year.

One of the biggest engineering challenges was how to ensure safe, breathable air in the tunnel. The Holland Tunnel was the first tunnel with a ventilation system capable of handling automobile and truck exhaust. To design it, Holland worked with a team of experts from Yale, the University of Illinois and the U.S. Bureau of Mines. He also traveled to Europe in 1921 to study the ventilation systems of tunnels in England, Germany and Scotland.

Ultimately, Holland devised the ingenious system that is still in use today. On both the New York and New Jersey shores, he built two ten-story ventilation towers. These towers house eighty-four giant fans. Some of the fans blow fresh air into the tunnel through ducts along the roadway surface, while others suck out the polluted air through ducts in the ceiling. Others are kept in reserve for emergencies. Together, these fans pump four million cubic feet of air per minute through the two-duct system, enough to completely replace all the air in the tunnel with fresh air every ninety seconds (forty-two times per hour). Holland's ventilation system would go on to be used in tunnels around the world.

Unfortunately, the project took a toll on Holland's health. The compression and decompression associated with descending into the tunnel and returning to the surface, often several times a day, did his weak heart no good. The worry and strain of the job became too much for him, and Holland suffered a nervous breakdown. In the fall of 1924, Holland went to the Battle Creek Sanitarium, run by Dr. John Harvey Kellogg, for

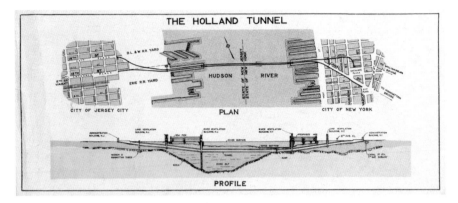

Map of routes to the Holland Tunnel. *New York Public Library Digital Collections.*

a rest. There, he suffered a heart attack and died on October 27, 1924, at the age of forty-one.

Holland's death came two days before the two crews digging the north tunnel—from both the New York and New Jersey sides—were scheduled to "hole through" or meet in the middle of the Hudson River. The celebration that had been planned to mark the occasion (including broadcasting the "holing through" on radio station WOR as President Coolidge touched off the detonation from the White House) was canceled out of respect for Holland. Two weeks later, the Hudson River Vehicular Tunnel was renamed the Holland Tunnel in his honor.[195]

It took another three years to complete construction. Holland's first replacement, Milton Freeman, died of pneumonia soon after taking on the role. It was left to Ole Singstad, who later went on to design the Lincoln Tunnel, the Queens-Midtown Tunnel and the Brooklyn-Battery (Hugh Carey) Tunnel, to complete the project.

OPENING THE HOLLAND TUNNEL

To great fanfare, the Holland Tunnel formally opened at 4:55 p.m. on November 12, 1927. Thousands gathered on each side of the river to hear speeches, and President Calvin Coolidge symbolically opened the tunnels from his yacht by turning a golden telegraph key that parted two large American flags draped over the entrances to the tunnel. This same key, which *Time* magazine called "the golden lever of the Presidential telegraphic instrument,"[196] had been used by President Wilson to explode the final charge on the Panama Canal in 1915.

Holland Tunnel. *Used with permission from the Museum of the City of New York.*

FUN FACT Concerns about carbon monoxide ventilation persisted throughout the project.* Port Authority chairman Eugenius Outerbridge *(see entry on Outerbridge)* promised that "if the ventilation...method proposed for the Canal Street tunnel should unexpectedly prove to be inadequate, the investment in this tunnel would not be lost; it would be entirely practicable to install moving platforms in this tunnel and to avoid the ventilation question altogether."†

---

* Editorial, N.Y. Times (Jan. 23, 1924).

† E.H. Outerbridge, Ventilating the Tunnel, Letter to the N.Y. Times (Jan. 25, 1924).

For the first two hours, the tunnel was open for pedestrian traffic only. Twenty thousand people, eager to make the "trip from shore to shore afoot," walked the entire 1.5-mile length of the tunnel. Acting like excited children, pedestrians sang and shouted to hear the echo, shook hands across the state line and generally enjoyed themselves.[197]

The first car to enter the Holland Tunnel at 12:01 a.m. on November 13 from Manhattan carried chairmen of the New York State Bridge and Tunnel Commission. The second carried Clifford Holland's widow. The first automobile accident in the Holland Tunnel occurred at 1:15 a.m. on November 13, roughly an hour after it opened.[198]

On that first day, 51,694 vehicles traveled through the tunnel, with 340 traveling through the north tube in the first hour. Although early plans had contemplated pedestrians[199] and horse-drawn vehicles, except during rush hour,[200] by the time the Holland Tunnel opened, both horse-drawn vehicles and pedestrians were prohibited entirely.[201]

When the Holland Tunnel opened in 1927, the toll was $0.50 per car in both directions, with buses paying $1.00 and trucks paying up to $2.00 depending on tonnage.[202] Today, those figures range from $11.75 to $16.00 for cars and up to $66.00 for trucks (larger trucks are not permitted in the Holland Tunnel).[203] The original plan was that the tunnel would become free after the tolls paid off the cost of construction. However, that option was long abandoned. In 1970, the Port Authority of New York and New Jersey switched to one-way tolls, and now those tolls are collected entirely by E-ZPass. More than fifteen million vehicles use the Holland Tunnel each year.

The Holland Tunnel was formally designated a National Historic Civil and Mechanical Engineering Landmark on May 2, 1984, and a National Historic Landmark in 1993.

FUN FACT Holland's mathematical calculations were so accurate that the two ends of the north tube met within a fraction of an inch (one centimeter) of each other.*

---

* Report of the New York State Bridge and Tunnel Commission to the Governor and Legislature of the State of New York (Mar. 20, 1925)

PART III

PARKS AND RECREATION

Chapter 1

WILLIAM CULLEN BRYANT

THE AUTHOR OF AMERICA

Bryant Park was named after author and poet William Cullen Bryant (1794–1878), the longtime editor of the *New York Evening Post*.

EARLY LIFE

William Cullen Bryant was born in Cummington, Massachusetts, on November 3, 1794, to Peter Bryant and Sarah Snell Bryant. He was one of seven children. His father, Peter, was a doctor who served in the Massachusetts legislature. A man of modest means, he encouraged his son's interest in reading and poetry. Bryant's aunt (his father's sister) Charity had a lifelong intimate partnership with Sylvia Drake that Bryant later described as "companions for life" in a "union no less sacred to them than the tie of marriage."[204]

William Cullen Bryant. *Photo by Mathew Benjamin Brady, Wikimedia Commons.*

At sixteen, Bryant was admitted to Williams College as a sophomore. Unfortunately, strained family finances forced him to leave after a single year. Williams nevertheless claims Bryant as an alumnus, and one of the college's residence halls is named in his honor.

Bryant's first poem, "Thanatopsis," was published when he was seventeen years old. Although he aspired to be a poet, Bryant decided to become a

*James Russell Lowell, A Fable for Critics (1848).

lawyer to support himself. He was admitted to the Massachusetts bar in 1815 and practiced law in Great Barrington until 1825. He nevertheless continued to write poetry and regularly published in the *North American Review*.

In 1821, Bryant married Frances Fairchild. Together, they had two daughters.

Bryant soon moved his family to New York City, where he abandoned law to return to writing. He wrote novels and poems and rapidly became an editor and co-owner of the *New York Evening Post*, a paper that claimed Alexander Hamilton and Archibald Gracie as founders. Bryant would spend the next fifty years as editor-in-chief of the *Post*.

POLITICS

At the *Post*, Bryant built a reputation as a social reformer—he defended the rights of religious minorities and immigrants and championed the rights of workers to form labor unions. He was a radical advocate for the rights of common people. But most of all, Bryant was an ardent abolitionist. He began speaking out against slavery and its expansion into the territories in the 1830s. He opposed the annexation of Texas on the grounds that it meant "the extension and perpetuation of slavery."[205]

After the *Dred Scott* decision, Bryant wrote a series of editorials excoriating the opinion as a "superficial and shallow" misreading of the Constitution, lamenting that "wherever our flag floats, it is the flag of slavery."[206] He called the Fugitive Slave Act "the most ruffianly act ever authorized by a deliberative assembly."[207]

Bryant was a strong early backer of Abraham Lincoln. Indeed, when Lincoln came to New York to give his "Right Makes Might" speech at Cooper Union (*see entry on Cooper*), Bryant introduced him as "an eminent citizen of the West," adding, to great applause, "These children of the West, my friends, form a living bulwark against the advance of Slavery, and from them is recruited the vanguard of the armies of liberty."[208]

Once Lincoln was elected president, Bryant continually pressed for immediate emancipation of all those who were enslaved. Bryant was president of the Emancipation League, whose mission was "to bring

An 1848 Free Soil banner. *Nathaniel Currier firm, Wikimedia Commons.*

FUN FACT In 1848, Bryant helped form the Free Soil Party, whose slogan was "Free Soil, Free Labor, Free Speech, Free Men." The party's goal was to block expansion of slavery, and it counted Frederick Douglass and Walt Whitman among its members. Former president Martin Van Buren ran as the Free Soil candidate against slave-owning Whig Zachary Taylor and proslavery Democrat Lewis Cass. Taylor won the presidency, but Van Buren received more than 10 percent of the vote and finished second in three northern states.

about emancipation throughout the whole land" and to repeal all laws recognizing the existence of slavery anywhere in United States territory.[209] Together with Peter Cooper and others, Bryant persuaded Congress to create the Freedman's Savings Bank and Trust Company to ensure that Black Union soldiers and freed enslaved people could save their wages and accumulate wealth.[210]

ARTS AND LETTERS

For half a century, Bryant was at the center of New York City's literary and art world. He was president of the American Art Union and a member of the Sketch Club and the National Academy. He chaired the Astor House (*see entry on Astor*) celebration for Robert Burns's 100th birthday.[211] He was friends with poets Elizabeth Barrett and Robert Browning. Bryant was closely associated with the Hudson River School of Art and was close friends with painter Thomas Cole.

FUN FACT Bryant lived through nineteen United States presidencies, from George Washington to Rutherford B. Hayes.

Bryant Park. *Photo by Jean-Christophe Benoist, Wikimedia Commons.*

Bryant was passionate about New York's cultural institutions. He was a vocal advocate for the creation of Central Park, as well as a leading proponent of the Metropolitan Museum of Art. He helped found the New York Medical College. At one point, Bryant was president of the New York Homeopathic Society.

In 1878, Bryant gave a speech at the unveiling of a bust honoring Italian revolutionary Giuseppe Mazzini. As he was returning home, he fell and hit his head. For the next two weeks, Bryant struggled to recover. Newspapers gave daily updates on his condition.[212] He died without recovering consciousness. Bryant was eighty-four years old. As news of Bryant's death spread, flags flew at half-mast across the City.[213] His funeral at All Souls Church was jammed with a who's who of New York.[214] In 1884, Reservoir Square, located between 5th and 6th Avenues at 40th through 42nd Street, was renamed Bryant Park in his honor.

Today, Bryant Park is one of the busiest public spaces in the world. It hosts a seasonal skating rink, a carousel, al fresco dining and scores of activities.

FUN FACT In 1858, while Bryant and his wife were in Paris, the New York legislature elected Bryant a regent to the University of the State of New York. Bryant only learned of his appointment from the newspaper. He expressed surprise at "the favorable opinion of so respected a public body, manifested in so spontaneous a manner, without the least solicitation on the part of my friends,"[*] but declined the appointment,[†] citing his "aversion to any form of public life."[‡]

---

[*] Bryant Letter to John Bigelow, July 9, 1858, The Letters of William Cullen Bryant 1858–1864 at 64–65 (William Cullen Bryant II and Thomas G. Voss, eds. 1984).
[†] Annual Report of the Regents of the State of New York, Vol. 102 at 278 (1889).
[‡] Bryant Letter to John Bigelow, supra. Note 233.

Among its other attractions, Bryant Park is home to the first major New York City monument to honor a woman. Dedicated in 1912, the Josephine Shaw Lowell Memorial Fountain is named for social worker and reformer Josephine Shaw Lowell.

Chapter 2

SHIRLEY CHISHOLM

UNBOUGHT AND UNBOSSED

The Shirley Chisholm State Park is named after Shirley Chisholm (1924–2005), the first Black woman elected to the United States Congress.

Early Life

Shirley Chisholm announcing her candidacy for the House of Representatives. *Library of Congress.*

Shirley Anita St. Hill Chisholm was born in Brooklyn on November 30, 1924. She was one of four children. During the Depression, her parents, Charles and Ruby St. Hill, struggled to support their family—her father worked in a factory making burlap bags, her mother as a seamstress and domestic worker. As a result, five-year-old Chisholm, along with her three sisters, went to live with her maternal grandmother in Barbados. Chisholm returned to Brooklyn at age eleven but kept her West Indian accent for the rest of her life. Chisholm's father, Charles, was a passionate follower of Marcus Garvey. As a child, Chisholm was immersed in political discussions about racial and economic inequality—perspectives that would ultimately shape her political career.

An academic standout in high school, Chisholm was offered full-tuition scholarships to Vassar and Oberlin. But the costs of room and board put these schools beyond the reach of Chisholm's family. She instead attended Brooklyn College, majoring in sociology and Spanish. On campus, Chisholm quickly became politically active, joining the Delta Sigma Theta sorority and the Harriet Tubman Society. With her fellow students, Chisholm advocated for ending the poll tax, for better treatment of Black military service members and for adding a class in Black history to Brooklyn College's curriculum.

Chisholm graduated with honors in 1946. Unfortunately, her employment opportunities were limited by the era's pervasive gender and racial discrimination. She ultimately found work in early childhood education and spent the next two decades building a successful career in that field. She ended this phase of her life holding a master's degree in elementary education from Columbia and overseeing multiple daycares as a consultant to the City of New York.

In 1949, she married Conrad Chisholm. The couple had no children. Chisholm and Conrad divorced in 1977. Soon after, Chisholm remarried, to Arthur Harwick Jr., a former colleague from the New York State Assembly.[215]

State Politics

During the late 1950s, Chisholm immersed herself in local Brooklyn politics. In 1960, she helped cofound the interracial Unity Democratic Club to take on Brooklyn's entrenched political bosses. An indefatigable campaigner, Chisholm knocked on thousands of doors as part of a Unity Club strategy to oust the all-white, all-male leadership of the local political machine. Their success sent shock waves through the state.

In 1964, Chisholm amplified those shock waves when she ran for the New York State Assembly over the objections of party bosses. Despite gendered pushback from hecklers demanding whether she made her husband breakfast before campaigning,[216] Chisholm won the election handily, becoming the second Black woman elected to the assembly—the first was Bessie Buchanan, who represented the Twelfth Assembly District in Harlem from 1955 to 1962.

As assemblywoman from the Fifty-Fifth Assembly District, Chisholm earned a reputation for always doing her homework and for being unafraid of debate.[217] She was very popular with her constituents and had no trouble winning three elections in four years (due to state reapportionment). She sponsored legislation providing unemployment insurance to domestic workers and protecting teachers from being fired for taking maternity leave.

CONGRESS

In 1968, a federal court ordered New York to redraw Brooklyn's congressional map to comply with the Voting Rights Act. This created a new Twelfth Congressional District designed to give representation to Bedford-Stuyvesant's overwhelmingly Black community.[218] Once again, the party bosses didn't want Chisholm to run. And once again, Chisholm refused to be deterred. Running on the slogan "Unbought and Unbossed," Chisholm traveled the district in a sound truck announcing, "Ladies and Gentlemen… this is fighting Shirley Chisholm coming through." She narrowly won the Democratic primary, defeating the party-endorsed candidates.

In the general election that fall, Chisholm faced off against James Farmer, a former Freedom Rider and cofounder of the Committee on Racial Equality (CORE). Chisholm and Farmer had similar stances on housing, employment, education and the Vietnam War. Farmer quickly framed the race in gendered terms. Denigrating Chisholm as "a little schoolteacher," Farmer asserted that the district needed "a man's voice in Washington."[219] Echoing this sexist tone, the *New York Times* characterized the race as between "Farmer and a Woman," not even bothering to include Chisholm's name in the headline.[220]

Chisholm pushed back aggressively, portraying Farmer as a Manhattanite carpetbagger. Using her fluent Spanish, she courted the district's Latinx population. Moreover, Chisholm had the advantage of being the Democratic candidate in this heavily Democratic district, while Farmer ran on the Liberal and Republican lines. On election day, Chisholm won handily, beating Farmer with 67 percent of the vote.

Chisholm's arrival in the House shook that "august body to its foundations."[221] Rather than

FUN FACT Chisholm's most lasting state legislative legacy was the New York SEEK initiative, which helps low-income students attend college.* One of SEEK's first partners was Chisholm's alma mater, Brooklyn College. Today, there are eleven SEEK programs across CUNY, as well as similar programs at SUNY and the state's independent colleges.

* Leslie Burger, SEEK Program 1967–68 Annual Report, available from the CUNY Digital History Archive, cdha.cuny.edu.

Shirley Chisholm's 1968 congressional campaign. *Courtesy of Special Collections and University Archives, Rutgers University Libraries.*

hewing to the tradition that freshman representatives "be seen and not heard,"[222] "Fighting Shirley Chisholm" immediately began making waves. The House's leadership had initially assigned her to the House Agricultural Subcommittee on Forestry and Rural Villages. This assignment reflected both Chisholm's junior status and the influence of southern white legislators looking to blunt her power. Chisholm publicly bucked what she called the "petrified, sanctified system of seniority,"[223] demanding a committee assignment more relevant to her Brooklyn constituents.[224] It worked. Chisholm was quickly reassigned to Veterans Affairs.[225]

In her first weeks in Congress, Chisholm co-sponsored bills to disband the House Un-American Activities Committee and to create a national holiday to honor the Reverend Martin Luther King. Her first House speech decried the Vietnam War and announced her opposition to any defense bill that funded the war.

Chisholm quickly became a national figure. Throughout the 1970s, repeated Gallup polls named her as one of America's ten most admired women. In 1971, she was a founding member of the Congressional Black Caucus. A few years later, Chisholm joined forces with fellow New Yorker Bella Abzug to organize the Congressional Women's Caucus. Toward the end of her career, Chisholm helped found the National Political Caucus of Black Women.

In her second term, the House leadership assigned Chisholm to the Education and Labor Committee. There, she made her mark as a leading voice for women and children. Chisholm sponsored legislation to increase federal funding for daycare facilities, helped pass Title IX (which banned gender discrimination in education) and was instrumental in overriding

President Ford's veto to pass the National School Lunch Bill. At her retirement, Chisholm credited her constituent Rabbi Menachem M. Schneerson, the Lubavitcher Rebbe, for advice that inspired both her collaboration with Kansas senator Robert Dole to expand the federal food stamps program and her sponsorship of the WIC program that provides supplemental nutrition to poor women and their babies.[226] Chisholm remained on the Education and Labor Committee until 1977, when she joined the powerful Rules Committee—the first Black woman and second woman to serve on this committee.

FUN FACT In objecting to her Forestry and Rural Villages assignment, Chisholm quipped, "Apparently all they know here in Washington about Brooklyn is that a tree grew there."*

* Mrs. Chisholm Is Elected to a Veteran's Committee, N.Y. Times (Feb. 19, 1969).

Chisholm was reelected seven times and served her Brooklyn district for fourteen years. In 1982, Chisholm decided not to seek an eighth term.[227] She was succeeded by Major Owens, who became known as "the Librarian" in Congress.

RUNNING FOR PRESIDENT

In 1972, Chisholm ran for president in the Democratic primary—becoming the first Black person and second woman to do so on a major party platform (the first was Margaret Chase Smith, who ran as a Republican in 1964). Once again, candidate Chisholm received a frosty welcome from the party's powers that be, including many of her fellow Black caucus members who had hoped to coalesce around a Black male candidate. Everyone told her that her campaign was not serious. In the *Wall Street Journal*, Norman Mailer characterized her campaign as "quixotic." But Chisholm refused to be sidelined. She truly lived her most famous saying: "If they don't give you a seat at the table, bring a folding chair."[228]

FUN FACT During Chisholm's presidential run, newspapers ran stories marveling that Conrad Chisholm was "willingly standing in the shadows" to support his wife.*

* Conrad Chisholm Content to Be the Candidate's Husband, Sarasota Journal (Feb. 29, 1972).

Chisholm survived multiple assassination attempts as she campaigned across the country. She had to sue to participate in the televised primary debates. Although she did not win any primaries, she went to the Democratic National Convention with 152 delegates (roughly 10 percent of the total).

Shirley Chisholm's presidential campaign poster, N.G. Slater Corporation, 1972. *Wikimedia Commons.*

Shirley Chisholm died of a stroke in 2005. She was eighty years old.

In 2014, the U.S. Post Office issued a commemorative Shirley Chisholm stamp. The next year, President Obama posthumously awarded her the Presidential Medal of Freedom. New York City commissioned a forty-foot monument honoring Chisholm for Brooklyn's Prospect Park.[229] In 2019, the Shirley Chisholm State Park opened in Brooklyn. Alongside Jamaica Bay, the 407-acre park has miles of marked trails, a pier for picnicking and fishing and a commemorative mural honoring Chisholm.

Chapter 3

BILLIE JEAN KING

CHAMPION OF THE COURTS

T he U.S. Open is held at the Billie Jean King National Tennis Center in Flushing Meadows Park.

FAMILY LIFE

Billie Jean King.
Wikimedia Commons.

Billie Jean King was born in Long Beach, California, on November 22, 1943, the first child of Betty Jerman Moffit and Bill Moffit. Always a talented athlete, she began playing baseball and softball as a young child. At age eleven, she took up tennis in part because her conservative Methodist parents wanted her to play a "more ladylike" sport. To raise money to purchase her own racket ($8.29), King swept sidewalks. Her family was not wealthy, and tennis was then a country club sport. The cost of tennis lessons was far beyond her working-class family's means. But the determined King found a teacher offering free tennis lessons in a neighborhood park. From an early age, King was a feminist and gender equality advocate. She got into trouble for wearing shorts rather than the tennis dresses expected of female players.

In 1965, Billie Jean married her college classmate and fellow tennis player Larry King. King always credited Larry for making her into a feminist by underscoring that as a mediocre men's player, he was treated far better than she was, even though she was a world champion. After their marriage, Larry encouraged King to pursue tennis full time.

FUN FACT King's younger brother Randy Moffit was also a professional athlete, pitching for the San Francisco Giants and other teams.

In 1981, King was outed as a lesbian when her paramour, Marilyn Barnett, brought a palimony suit against her. That made King the first openly gay female athlete, albeit not intentionally. The Kings' marriage survived the publicity of the lawsuit, but the couple divorced amicably in 1987. In 2018, King married her doubles partner, Ilana Kloss, in a ceremony performed by former New York City mayor David Dinkins.[230]

TENNIS CAREER

In 1959, the fifteen-year-old King made her Grand Slam debut at the U.S. Championship. She lost in the first round. Two years later, King missed her high school graduation to play at Wimbledon. She and her partner, Helen Hantze, won the Wimbledon women's doubles title. King was ranked the number-three women's tennis player in the United States. Nevertheless, she could not get a sports scholarship to college because no colleges offered athletic scholarships for women.[231] It was only with the passage of Title IX in 1972 that colleges began offering women athletic scholarships and funding women's sports programs.

By 1966, King was the number-one women's tennis player in the world. She won the Wimbledon singles championship three years in a row. Two years later, King won both the singles and doubles Wimbledon championships. But she was paid a fraction of what the male winner received.

Fed up with unequal pay and unequal treatment, King joined with eight other women's tennis players to launch their own tour in 1970.[232] The players, known as the Original Nine, took a big risk. The male-dominated U.S. Lawn Tennis Association (now the U.S. Tennis Association) responded by threatening to ban them from major tournaments. But the success of the tour—which was called the Virginia Slims circuit by its sponsor, Phillip Morris—forced professional tennis to begin confronting its record of sexism and gender disparity.

In 1973, Billie Jean King and the Original Nine started the Women's Tennis Association (WTA). Their goal was to organize tournaments that would offer female players better prize money and more opportunity.[233] Today, the WTA is the governing body for women's tennis. The WTA now consists of more than 1,800 players representing eighty-five countries.[234] In 2021, the Original Nine were inducted into the International Tennis Hall of Fame.[235]

Billie Jean King and Bobby Riggs. *Wikimedia Commons.*

Also in 1973, King played the world's most famous exhibition tennis match against Bobby Riggs—the so-called Battle of the Sexes. King, who was twenty-nine years old, faced off against the much older Riggs in the Houston Astrodome before a live audience of more than thirty thousand spectators. The match was televised globally to more than ninety million viewers—making it the most watched U.S. tennis match ever.

The stakes were high, much higher than the $100,000 prize money. Riggs, a self-proclaimed male chauvinist pig, had loudly boasted, "There's no way that broad can beat me."[236] King knew she was playing for all women demanding equality and respect in a male-dominated world—a risky political choice but one she thought necessary. Pre-match betting heavily favored Riggs, who showed up for the match in a jacket emblazoned with "Sugar Daddy."[237] King trounced him, beating Riggs in straight sets 6–4, 6–3, 6–3.[238] After the match, Riggs hopped the net and reportedly whispered, "I underestimated you" to the victorious King.[239]

The match brought attention to the women's movement and the struggle for gender equality, a cause that King had long advocated. In the run-up to the match, King announced she would boycott the U.S. Open unless male and female players were offered the same prize money. As a result, the U.S. Open became the first major tennis tournament to offer equal

FUN FACT About her win, the *New York Times* wrote, "In a single tennis match, Billie Jean King was able to do more for the cause of women than most feminists can achieve in a lifetime."* King herself quipped, "I know that when I die, nobody at my funeral will be talking about me. They'll all just be standing around telling each other where they were the night I beat Bobby Riggs."†

---

* The Troubles and Triumph of Billie Jean King, N.Y. Times (May 6, 1981).
† Susan Ware, Game, Set, Match 1 ((2011).

Billie Jean King National Tennis Center. *Wikimedia Commons.*

prize money. (For perspective, FIFA, soccer's governing body, still pays women World Cup champions about five cents on the dollar compared to men.) King wound up testifying before Congress about gender discrimination and unequal pay and marched for equal rights alongside New York representative Bella Abzug and Gloria Steinem.

Over the course of her career, King won thirty-nine Grand Slams in singles, doubles and mixed doubles tennis. Her career win–loss record was 52–4. She retired in 1983. At this writing, King still holds the record for the most Wimbledon victories across all events (tied with Martina Navratilova).[240] In 2006, the U.S. Tennis Association renamed the National Tennis Center in Flushing Meadow Park in her honor. The U.S. Open is held in the Billie Jean King National Tennis Center.

King served as a director of the Elton John Aids Foundation and the National AIDs Fund. In 2014, King and her wife founded the Billie Jean King Leadership Initiative to combat workplace discrimination and inequality. The BJKLI fights for equality for all, regardless of race, gender, religion, ability or sexual orientation.[241]

King has been honored repeatedly for the way she transformed women's tennis and women's athletics more generally. She was the first woman ever named as *Sports Illustrated* sportsperson of the year. *Time* made her its Person of the Year in 1975. *Life* named her to its list of the "100 Most Important Americans." In 2019, ESPN established the Billie Jean King Youth Leadership Award to recognize young athletes who use sports to improve their communities.[242] In 2021, *Sports Illustrated* gave King the Muhammad Ali Legacy Award.

In 2009, President Barack Obama awarded King the Presidential Medal of Freedom in honor of her work championing gender equality in sports and all areas of public life and for her work on behalf of the LGBTQIA+ community.

FUN FACT At five feet, four and a half inches, King is the shortest player to have ever won a Grand Slam in tennis.

Chapter 4

WILLIAM SHEA

THE MAN IN THE ROOM

S hea Stadium, home to the New York Mets from 1964 to 2008, was named after William Alfred Shea (1907–1991), the man credited with bringing National League baseball back to New York City after the Giants and Dodgers abandoned the city.

FAMILY LIFE

William Shea. *Photo by William C. Greene,* World Telegram *staff photographer, Wikimedia Commons.*

William Shea was born in New York City on June 21, 1907, to Olive L. (Martin) and Ashley P. Shea.[243] Shea attended George Washington High School in Manhattan's Washington Heights. He entered New York University on a basketball scholarship but soon transferred to Georgetown, where he played basketball and football. He earned his BA in 1930 and a law degree in in 1931. After law school, Shea moved to Brooklyn, where he worked for the State Department of Banking. He became active in the local Democratic Party but always behind the scenes, never as a candidate. Between his job, which involved liquidating the assets of failed banks and insurance companies, and his campaigning, Shea built up a network of influence that prompted the description that he was New York City's "most experienced power broker, its premier matchmaker."[244]

In 1938, Shea married May Shaw. Together, they had three children.

Law Practice

Shea wielded tremendous influence as "the unofficial chairman of the state's unofficial permanent government,"[245] made up of wealthy, connected (white) men. He was confidant to two New York governors, Nelson A. Rockefeller and Hugh L. Carey, and advisor to New York City mayors Robert F. Wagner, John V. Lindsay and Abraham D. Beame. He was widely known as the sort of lawyer whom powerful people "could rely upon as a go-between."[246] Some joked that Shea had no idea where the courthouse was,[247] and even Shea's law partner Morton Gould described him as "incapable of parsing a sentence" but still able to "get his message across."[248]

The law firm Shea co-founded, Shea and Gould, was one of the most influential firms in the City. At its high point, the firm employed well over two hundred lawyers. It was known for its aggressive, "spit in your eye" culture.[249] Despite claiming that his motto was "never get even,"[250] Shea prided himself on the firm's bare-knuckled wrangling. He proudly declared, "We're not statesmen....We ain't white shoe."[251] However, others viewed the firm's practices of "getting around the law without breaking the law" as unsavory, characterizing the firm as "a factory of legal graft."[252] The firm imploded in 1994.

Baseball

It was in New York City baseball that Shea left his biggest mark. In 1957, both the New York Giants and the Brooklyn Dodgers left New York. Faced with this catastrophe, Mayor Richard Wagner appointed Shea as chair of a committee of "prominent citizens" tasked with bringing a National League team back to New York City. Shea first tried to entice an existing team to relocate to New York. When those overtures failed, Shea proposed creating

FUN FACT Shea's sister Olive Gloria Shea had a brief career as a B-list actress.* She appeared in ten movies with titles like *Money Means Nothing* and *The Dude Bandit*. In 1938, she married her childhood sweetheart, Vice Admiral Robert J. Stroh, a decorated World War II hero. Together, they had two children.

* Gloria Shea Was a Ziegfeld Girl, Universal Weekly (May 13, 1933).

Shea Stadium. *Photo by Metsfan84, Wikimedia Commons.*

a third major baseball league—the Continental League—with eight new teams to be located in New York, Buffalo, Denver, Minneapolis, Toronto, Atlanta, Houston and Dallas. This proposal was widely viewed as political gamesmanship but was effective nonetheless. The National League agreed to create two expansion teams, one of which was the New York Mets. The main financial backer of the Continental League, Joan Whitney Payson, niece of Gertrude Vanderbilt Whitney (*see entry on Whitney*) became the first owner of the Mets. Shea was reportedly offered a 25 percent ownership stake in the Mets as payment for his effort, but he turned it down.

Shea Stadium was built on the Willets Point site selected by Robert Moses, who spearheaded a campaign to have the new stadium named after Shea. In 1964, when New York in fact named the stadium after him, Shea predicted that it would be renamed fifteen minutes after he died. But Shea's prediction proved false. Shea stadium was never renamed. Instead, in 2008, nearly twenty years after Shea's 1991 death, Shea Stadium was demolished. In building its replacement, the Mets retired the Shea name and sold naming rights for the new stadium to Citigroup for $400 million. The Mets currently play at Citi Field, which has a pedestrian bridge named after Shea.

FUN FACT Of the eight cities Shea proposed as candidates for teams in the Continental League, seven now have thriving expansion teams (and the eighth, Buffalo, has a popular AAA team). Indeed, the fourteen teams admitted to the Major Leagues since 1960 owe their existence to Shea's initial advocacy, which paved the way for expansion teams.

At its opening, the multiuse Shea Stadium, which did double duty for both baseball and football, was hailed as "one of the most modern and beautiful sports facilities in the world."[253] The stadium also hosted boxing matches, soccer games, pro wrestling events and religious

FUN FACT Even though Shea was instrumental in bringing the Mets to New York City and threw out the first-ever ceremonial first pitch at Shea Stadium, he was also a lifelong friend to Yankees owner George Steinbrenner.

gatherings. However, the stadium's awkward design rapidly became obsolete. By the time the last game was played there in 2008, the *New York Times* lamented, "Nobody has ever called Shea Stadium a cathedral."[254] However, despite its awkward architecture, Shea Stadium was a hallowed venue for rock music and the birthplace of arena concerts. Shea Stadium played host to two iconic Beatles concerts, as well as blockbuster shows by the Who, the Police and the Rolling Stones, among others.

Shea also helped bring a hockey team, the New York Islanders, to the new Nassau Coliseum; was part owner of the Washington Redskins; and helped create the Superbowl. He served on the boards of multiple insurance companies and was awarded honorary degrees from Georgetown, St. Johns University, Long Island University and St. Francis College.

Shea died in 1991, two years after suffering an incapacitating stroke. He was eighty-four.

Chapter 5

LOULA LASKER

SOCIALIST AT THE PIERRE HOTEL

L asker Rink and Pool, located at 108th Street in Central Park, is named after Loula D. Lasker (1886–1961), a New York City social worker and activist.

FAMILY LIFE

Loula Davis Lasker was born in Galveston, Texas, on February 7, 1884, to parents Morris K. Lasker and Nettie Heidenheimer. Morris was a Jewish immigrant from Prussia. Despite professing pro-Union sentiments, he was conscripted to fight for the South during the Civil War. After the war, Morris spent time as an itinerant peddler before settling in Galveston, where he became a prominent and wealthy merchant and banker. Nettie was from a wealthy New York family. One of eight children, Loula was a debutante in Galveston's Jewish society in 1909.[255]

Throughout her life, Loula was a fierce advocate for social justice and equality, following in the footsteps of her father, Morris. Indeed, Morris was the second mill owner in the country to adopt an eight-hour workday, and Morris prided himself on paying his workers a

Loula Lasker. *Photo used with permission from the American Jewish Historical Society and Hadassah, the Women's Zionist Organization of America, Inc.*

fair wage.[256] Loula's older brother Albert Davis Lasker was a pioneer in the field of marketing, creating *reason why* advertising techniques.[257] Albert used his marketing skills to help elect Warren G. Harding—the first use of *reason why* advertising in a presidential campaign.[258]

PROFESSIONAL LIFE

Lasker graduated from Vassar College in 1909. She also held a graduate degree in social work from New York University. In 1916, Lasker moved to New York City, where she became a leading socialist intellectual and activist. Among her many public service posts, she worked for the Bureau of Philanthropic Research and the American Red Cross. In 1921, she was appointed to the United States Immigration Commissioner's Advisory Panel focusing on welfare conditions at immigration stations. The panel's recommendations "revolutionized" care for immigrants on Ellis Island.[259] During that same period, she served as chair of the Commission on Immigrant Aid and Immigrant Education for the National Council of Jewish Women.

She spent twenty years as editor of *Survey* and *Survey Graphic* magazines, writing extensively on issues of race relations, refugee problems, immigration and urban planning. With her older sisters Etta and Florina, Lasker wrote a landmark report for the Bureau of Philanthropic Research called *Care and Treatment of the Jewish Blind in the City of New York.*

SOCIAL JUSTICE ADVOCACY

Lasker was a passionate advocate for social justice and a pioneer in the field of housing. She helped found the Citizens Housing and Planning Council (then called the Citizens Housing Council) and served as the organization's second chairperson.[260] She used this position to advocate for affordable, racially nondiscriminatory housing in New York City and for equitable access to parks and greenspaces.[261] A board member of the Union League, Lasker donated generously to campaigns "to prove that discrimination based on class, race, or religion has no place in the world."[262]

Lasker helped found the National Housing Conference and was a leading voice on the need for public housing. She served on the Planning Committee for the 1934 MOMA exhibit titled "Americans Can't Have Housing." Throughout her career, Lasker took many public stands against racial discrimination in housing—most notably her arguments against approval of Stuyvesant Town, in part because of its proposed racially exclusionary policies. Despite her sincere commitment to public and affordable housing, Lasker herself lived in luxury at the Pierre Hotel.

Lasker also served on the board for the League for Industrial Democracy, was vice president of the Union League and was a longtime board member of the American Civil Liberties Union. Lasker's mother, Nettie, left a bequest to be managed by Lasker and her sisters "for the benefit of women." They used the money to support Margaret Sanger's work on birth control and helped found the Birth Control Federation. Lasker's advertising mogul brother Albert later persuaded Sanger to change the name of the organization to Planned Parenthood.

A committed Zionist, Lasker was very active in Jewish institutions. She served on Hadassah's national board from 1949 until her death in 1961. She was elected as the organization's national vice president in 1960, after a stint on the Public Relations Committee. In this capacity, Lasker oversaw a network of medical and social service institutions.

Lasker was also an art collector—with a focus on modern art. At her death, she left an extensive collection that included works by Dalí, Monet, Renoir, Gauguin, Miró and Picasso. She left the bulk of her collection to the Bezalel Museum in Jerusalem. However, she left a Monet painting of *Parc Monceau, Paris* and Gauguin's *Ia Orana Maria* to the New York Metropolitan Museum of Art and Matisse's *Lemons Against a Fleur-de-lis Background* to MOMA. The Whitney, the Guggenheim, the Art Institute of Chicago and the National Gallery also received works from her collection.

Lasker died of a heart attack in 1961. She was seventy-two. Her will set up the Loula D. Lasker Foundation and created a trust fund for graduate study in housing and city planning. At the time, the Loula D. Lasker Fellowship in City Planning, Housing and Urban Development was viewed as a "breakthrough for training in the field."[263] Vassar has an endowed Loula D. Lasker Scholarship. Lasker and her sister Florina also endowed United Negro College Fund scholarships to fund graduate studies for Black women.[264]

Lasker Rink

Lasker Rink was the last of the Robert Moses–era large-scale recreation facilities built in Central Park with privately donated money. It cost $2.6 million to build. In her will, Lasker bequeathed $600,000 to help build the rink.

Lasker Rink. *Photo by Jim Henderson, Wikimedia Commons.*

Construction of the rink sparked major protests by Central Park preservationists. Indeed, the rink remains controversial with Central Park purists (the AIA calls it the park's "most disastrous" improvement),[265] as it interferes with park designer Frederick Law Olmsted's plan for a broad sylvan expanse to the Harlem Meer.

In recent years, the Lasker Rink has been operated by Donald Trump. As a result, the rink's website has the Trump name plastered all over it, and it is difficult to find the Lasker name. However, after the January 6, 2021 attack on the U.S. Capitol, Mayor de Blasio announced that the city was ending its contracts with the Trump Organization, including the contract to manage the Lasker Rink. The rink was demolished in 2021 and will be replaced with a new LEED Gold facility in 2024.

FUN FACT The Lasker Rink was the first combined outdoor swimming pool/ice skating rink ever constructed.[*]

* NYC Department of Parks, 30 Years of Progress: 1934–1964 www.nycgovparks.org/sub_about/parks_history/library/pdf/thirty_years_of_progress.pdf.

PART IV

NEIGHBORHOODS

Chapter 1

JOHN JACOB ASTOR

AMERICA'S FIRST MULTIMILLIONAIRE

The Queens neighborhood of Astoria was named after John Jacob Astor (1763–1848), a German immigrant who at his death was the wealthiest man in America.

John Jacob Astor, originally named Johann Jakob Astor, was born near Heidelberg, Germany, on July 17, 1763, to butcher Johann Jakob Astor and Maria Magdalena Vorfelder. He was the youngest of six children. His mother died when Astor was three. His father remarried and had another six children. In 1780, at the age of seventeen, Astor made his way to London, where his older brother George ran a successful musical instrument business. It was there that Astor anglicized his name.

Two months after the Treaty of Paris ended the Revolutionary War, Astor boarded the *North Carolina* and embarked for the United States at the urging of his brother Henry.[266] His plan was to import and sell George's musical instruments.[267] Astor traveled in steerage, with his best suit, a bit of money and several of his brother's flutes. Aboard ship, Astor allegedly met a furrier, who sparked Astor's interest in the lucrative fur trade. The journey was long and arduous, made more so because Astor's ship spent weeks locked in ice off the coast of Virginia. Astor eventually walked ashore over

John Jacob Astor. *Painting by John Wesley Jarvis, Wikimedia Commons.*

FUN FACT Astor's older brother Heinrich signed on to be a Hessian mercenary fighting for the British in the Revolutionary War. Almost as soon as he got to America, Heinrich changed his name to Henry and deserted his regiment. He opened a butcher shop in New York City.

the frozen sea ice. He arrived in Baltimore in March 1784. A chance encounter with a fellow German allowed him to sell his flutes easily. Astor used the money to join his brother in New York. Once in New York, Astor worked first as a delivery boy for a baker and then as an assistant to a fur dealer. Astor invested all his money in fur pelts, which he sold in England.[268]

On September 19, 1785, Astor married Sarah Cox Todd, his landlady's daughter. Together, they had eight children, three of whom died in infancy. Sarah's dowry allowed the couple to set up their own fur shop, and her family connections and social network helped forge the Astor trade empire.[269]

By the turn of the century, Astor was one of the leading figures in the fur trade. When President Jefferson's Trade Embargo Act of 1807 thwarted Astor's ongoing trade with Canada and China, Astor turned his attention instead to the Pacific coast. By the time Astor received a charter for the American Fur Company from the New York legislature in 1808,[270] he was already managing "an international empire that mixed furs, teas, and silks and penetrated markets on three continents."[271] The American Fur Company was notorious for selling alcohol to Indians despite clear federal law prohibiting such sales.

In a series of letters with President Jefferson, Astor pitched his commercial venture as a plan for expanding American influence across the North American continent. He sought a presidential stamp of approval for his plans to trade with the western Indians. Jefferson promised to lend the enterprise "every reasonable patronage and facility in the power of the Executive."[272] With Jefferson's approval, Astor formed the short-lived Pacific Fur Company as a wholly owned subsidiary of his American Fur Company.

Astor's scheme was to establish a string of trading posts along the Missouri and the Columbia Rivers. To that end, the Pacific Fur Company established the first United States settlement on the Pacific coast, Fort Astoria, and sent two expeditions westward: one overland and one by

FUN FACT After the British captured Fort Astoria during the War of 1812, the *New York Gazette* published a terse announcement that "the firm of the Pacific Fur Company is dissolved." Astor's expeditioners fled back to St. Louis. On the way, they discovered the South Pass through the Rocky Mountains—the route thousands of settlers later used to travel west.

sea. The overland Astor Expedition followed Lewis and Clark's route, while the second expedition sailed around Cape Horn. The two groups linked up at Fort Astoria in what is now Oregon.[273]

In 1816, Astor persuaded Congress to pass a law banning British citizens from trading in the American territories. By 1830, Astor had a near-total monopoly over the fur trade in the United States. Yet by 1834, Astor had sold his interests in the American Fur Company. That same year, Astor commissioned Washington Irving to write an official history of the Astor Expedition. Irving's book *Astoria, or Enterprise Beyond the Rockies* was published in 1836 and quickly became an international bestseller.

Astor parlayed his fur trade fortune into an even bigger fortune through real estate. He began buying land in 1789, a practice he continued until his death in 1848. During the panic of 1837, Astor bought up the holdings of countless small landowners, foreclosing on scores of mortgages in the process.

Over the ensuing decades, Astor amassed an astonishing real estate portfolio—his deeds and conveyances took up seven pages of the City's Index of Conveyances. He ultimately owned much of lower Manhattan and midtown,[274] including all of what would become Times Square.[275] At its peak, Astor's real estate empire generated roughly $200,000 a year in rent

THE FAMOUS OLD ASTOR HOUSE, BROADWAY AND VESEY STREET, OPPOSITE THE ENTRANCE TO THE PARK, AS IT APPEARED WHEN FIRST ERECTED IN 1842. THIS VIEW SHOWS WHAT A CHARMING SPOT WAS OBLITERATED WHEN THE POST OFFICE WAS ERECTED HERE

Astor House, Popular Graphic Arts. *Wikimedia Commons.*

(nearly $6 million in 2016 dollars). At his death, Astor was the world's fifth-richest man, with a fortune between $30 and $40 million[276] (roughly $1.24 billion in 2020 dollars). He was one of the richest Americans ever.[277]

In 1836, Astor branched out even further, opening Astor House, the first luxury hotel in New York City. Located at the corner of Broadway and Vesey Street, Astor House rapidly became the most famous hotel in America. Abraham Lincoln stayed there in 1860 when he visited New York and gave his famous Cooper Institute speech (*see entry on Cooper*).[278]

Astor was close friends with Archibald Gracie (*see entry on Gracie*) and was a frequent visitor at Gracie Mansion. Astor built his own country house nearby at what is now 87th Street and York Avenue. The house stood on an 11.3-acre parcel, with a view of the East River at Hells Gate.

Stephen A. Halsey, founder of the Astoria neighborhood of New York, proposed naming the town after John Jacob Astor in the hopes that Astor would make a large donation to a young ladies' seminary, which would also be named after him. Astor made the donation, but instead of the generous support Halsey had been hoping for, Astor donated only $500 to the Astoria Institute. Nevertheless, the "Act to Incorporate the Village of Astoria" passed the New York state legislature on April 12, 1839. Astor himself never visited Astoria, even though he could see it from his country house on the other side of the East River.

John Jacob Astor died in 1848. He was eighty-five years old. His friend Washington Irving served as one of his pallbearers.

For many people, Astor "symbolized...the obscenity of great wealth."[279] The narrator in Herman Melville's *Bartleby the Scrivener* loved to repeat John Jacob Astor's "round and orbicular" name because it "rings like unto bullion." Astor was generally considered "the most hated man in America,"[280] a sobriquet that passed on his death to Henry Frick. The *New York Herald* published Astor's will on the front page, as part of a broader call for taxes on landlords. In that will, Astor left $400,000 for the establishment of a reference library in New York. The Astor Library opened its

Astor Library, cartoon
by Chip. *Wikimedia
Commons.*

doors in 1854. Like the Lenox Library (*see entry on Lenox*), the Astor Library
was a reference library—its 100,000 books were not permitted to circulate.
Washington Irving, who had persuaded Astor to make the bequest, served
as the Astor Library's first president.[281] Astor's bequest specified that the
library was to be located at the corner of Lafayette Place and Art Street
(now Astor Place) and was "to be accessible at all
reasonable hours and times, for general use, free of
expense to persons resorting thereto, subject only to
such control and regulations, as the Trustees may
from time to time exercise and establish for general
convenience."[282] However, the Astor Library was
open only during daylight hours and had a reputation
for not welcoming working-class readers.[283] Critics
also decried the lack of a useful catalogue.[284]

In 1895, the Astor Library and the Lenox Library
combined with the Tilden Library to form the New
York Public Library. The new public library was
located on 5th Avenue and 42nd Street—the site of

FUN FACT The famous
marble lions that flank
the 5th Avenue entrance
to the New York Public
Library were originally
named Leo Astor and
Leo Lenox. During the
Depression, Mayor
LaGuardia renamed them
Patience and *Fortitude.*

the Croton Reservoir. The Astor Library building was sold to the Hebrew
Immigrant Aid Society, which used the building to process thousands of
new immigrants to New York City. In the 1960s, the Astor Library was the
first building saved from demolition under New York City's Landmarks
Preservation Law.[285] It is now home to the Joseph Papp Public Theater.

Astor's great-grandson John Jacob Astor IV was the wealthiest person to die on the *Titanic*. He left an estate of $100 million[286] (roughly $2.4 billion in 2020 dollars). His son Vincent Astor married Brooke Russell, to whom he left all his money. Despite her fabulous wealth, Brooke Russell Astor was the subject of a notorious case of elder abuse at the hands of her son by an earlier marriage.[287]

Chapter 2

GOWANUS

THE (MAYBE) SACHEM

The Gowanus Canal may or may not have been named after a Lenape or Canarsee sachem (chief).

In the 1600s, when the Dutch began settling Nieu Amsterdam, they were concentrated in the area they called Breuckelen (present-day Brooklyn), probably after a town in the Netherlands. At the time, the area was home to the Canarsee Indians. One of the first recorded references to the area by the name *Gowanus* was in an April 5, 1642 grant from Willem Kieft, then director-general of New Netherlands, to one Cornelius Lambersen Cool of "land on Long island called Gouwanes, previously occupied by Jan van Rotterdam and Thomas Beets."[288] Cornelius Cool did not live long after the transfer—a subsequent deed dated January 5, 1644, divided this land between Cool's widow and sons-in-law.[289] By 1645, Gouwanes had become a recognized boundary marker for deeds, as indicated in an "Indian deed" conveying land "from Kyned (Coney) island to Gouwanes."[290] From these references, it has been speculated that Gowanes was a Canarsee chief because "his name persisted as its title."[291] According to legend, Sachem Gowanes owned land south of Brueckelen, and that is why the creek, bay and region bore his name.[292] Despite a lack of evidence to support this claim, it has become "internet-true."[293] More recently, some historians instead suggest that instead of reflecting an actual person's landholdings, the name Gowanus was instead derived from Algonquin descriptive words used as place names.[294] Whether Gowanus takes its name from a person or a place description, its origin is clearly Algonquin.

Gowanus Canal. *Photo by King of Hearts, Wikimedia Commons.*

During the 1600s, the Gowanus area was a lush marsh, with many inlets and small creeks. The area's tidal wetlands and freshwater streams supported an abundance of fish, birds and other wildlife. Indeed, hard as it is to imagine today, the Dutch settlers' first export to Europe were enormous, platter-sized oysters harvested from Gowanus.[295] Under the direction of Peter Stuyvesant, enslaved African laborers built the first tide mill in Gowanus, and the power was used to grind corn. This mill was destroyed by the Continental army as they retreated across Gowanus Creek during the Battle of Brooklyn.

As the population of New York expanded, overexploitation dramatically reduced the previously abundant fish and oyster populations. Moreover, pollution from villages, including sewage, contaminated the waters, further reducing fish stocks and rendering the oysters inedible.

In 1849, the New York state legislature authorized the construction of the Gowanus Canal to connect the Port of New York with the Gowanus Bay and, ultimately, the Atlantic Ocean. One hundred feet wide and 1.8 miles long, the canal soon became one of the nation's busiest industrial waterways. Among the industrial facilities concentrated along the banks of the Gowanus Canal were oil refineries, manufactured gas plants (which turned coal into gas for use in electricity), paper mills, tanneries and chemical plants. These polluting facilities all used the Gowanus Canal as their dumping ground. Industrial pollutants, combined with stormwater runoff and raw sewage (the canal served as an open

FUN FACT In marketing materials for the new luxury condos lining the canal, this history of pollution and contamination morphs into "an exciting hub of industry and shipping, mirroring the ascendancy of New York City itself."*

———————————

* Gowanus, 365bond.com/ gowanus.

sewer in the 1860s), turned the canal into a fetid, stagnant pool. The bottom of the canal is lined with "black mayonnaise"—the colloquial name for more than a century's worth of toxic and contaminated sludge.[296] In 1877, the board of health declared the canal a public nuisance, and the ensuing decades saw numerous unsuccessful attempts to remedy the odor and pollution.

The stinking, discolored Gowanus Canal earned the nickname "Lavender Lake." By 1952, many, including the police who patrolled Gowanus by boat, considered the canal to be the River Styx of New York City—a region of the dead.[297] Indeed, there have been many, many headlines proclaiming "Body Found in Gowanus Canal."[298] Long considered a monument to urban blight, the canal was lined by abandoned buildings and vacant lots. It served as a dumping ground for tires, sewer overflows and other waste. Nearby residents considered the stinky,

FUN FACT In 2012, Superstorm Sandy's storm surge caused the Gowanus Canal to overflow its banks—sending contaminated water into nearby neighborhoods. Then–city councilmember Brad Lander advised his Gowanus Canal–area constituents, "Do not touch standing water in the area or any sediment or debris left by Gowanus flood-waters."*

* New York City Councilmember Brad Lander, Update on Gowanus Canal Flooding Issues (Oct. 29, 2012), bradlander.nyc/blog/2012/10/29/update-on-gowanus-canal-flooding-issues.

FREEKE'S MILLS WITH YELLOW MILLS IN THE DISTANCE
burnt on the 27 h of Aug.1776 while the Americans were retreating across Gowanus Creek.

Freeke's Mill. *Original from Thomas Warren, Historic and Antiquarian Scenes in Brooklyn and Its Vicinity 34 (1868).*

Busy Gowanus. *Photo from* Brooklyn Daily Eagle, *1901, courtesy of Brooklyn Public Library, Center for Brooklyn History.*

dirty waterway "a nasty showplace."[299] On occasion, a whale or dolphin wandered into the canal, usually with fatal results.

Today, the Gowanus Canal is lined by the gentrified Brooklyn neighborhoods, including Park Slope, Boerum Hill, Cobble Hill, Carroll Gardens and Red Hook. Thousands of people live within one block of the canal. Yet the canal remained one of the nation's most polluted waterways.

In 2010, the United States EPA designated the Gowanus Canal a Superfund site and added it to the National Priorities List. The listing came over the objections of then-mayor Bloomberg, who had instead advocated voluntary, more development-friendly cleanup. In 2013, the EPA finalized a cleanup plan for the Gowanus Canal, which is projected to last until well after 2029.[300] In the meantime, the EPA advises people to "minimize direct contact" with the canal's toxic waters. The cost of the cleanup is expected to exceed $1 billion. Nevertheless, the neighborhood is one of New York City's hottest real estate markets, with undeveloped sites selling for millions of dollars[301] and new apartments renting for thousands of dollars per month. At one new development, two-bedroom apartments rent for more than $5,000 per month.

FUN FACT A Whole Foods opened along the Gowanus in 2013, prompting some to tag Gowanus "Brooklyn's coolest superfund site."*

* Tiffany Yanetta, Live on the Scene at the Whole Foods Gowanus Opening! Racked N.Y. (Dec. 17, 2013) (quoting the Gowanus Canal Conservancy).

Chapter 3

ADRIAEN VAN DER DONCK

THE YOUNG SIR (YONKERS)

T he city of Yonkers takes its name from the nickname of Adriaen
Cornelissen van der Donck (1620–1655), the first lawyer in America,
who was commonly called *Jonkeer* or *Jonker* (Young Sir).[302]

FAMILY LIFE

Adriaen van der Donck.
Courtesy National Gallery of Art.

Adriaen van der Donck was born in Breda,
Netherlands, sometime between 1618 and 1620
to parents Cornelis Gijsbrechtszoon van der
Donck and Agatha van Bergen. As the son of
a relatively wealthy and well-connected family,
van der Donck had the opportunity to study at
Leiden University. He graduated in 1641 with a
degree in both civil and canon law. That same
year, Amsterdam merchant and cofounder of
the Dutch West Indies Company Kiliaen van
Rensselaer hired van der Donck to be the *schout*
(legal officer) for the Rensselaerswyck colony.
On May 17, 1641, van der Donck left for
New Netherlands armed with strict instructions from Rensselaer. He was
just twenty-one years of age.

Van der Donck was the first lawyer in New Netherlands.[303] As Rensselaer's schout, he was a combination sheriff and agent. In that role, van der Donck was tasked with managing the feudal estate for Rensselaer's profit and benefit. However, van der Donck's training at Leiden had been steeped in anti-feudal ideas.[304] As a result, he often sided with the settlers against van Rensselaer, making the employment relationship fraught. Nevertheless, van der Donck held his post for three years. During that period, van der Donck spent a great deal of his time roaming the Catskills and learning the languages and customs of the local Indian tribes.

In 1645, van der Donck married Mary Doughty, daughter of English Puritans Bridget and Reverend Francis Doughty. It is believed the van der Doncks did not have any children. The next year, van der Donck's house burned down, and he decided to leave the Rensselaer colony. By then, van der Donck's knowledge of Mohawk and Mohican was so well respected that New Netherlands director-general Willem Kieft asked his help in negotiating an end to a disastrous and brutal war between the Dutch and virtually all the tribes in the region. (The conflict was known as Kieft's War because it was his bad judgment and bellicosity that instigated the fighting.) As payment for his assistance, van der Donck received the large tract of land in present-day Westchester that bears his *nick*name, *Jonkeer*, or Yonkers. Thus, van der Donck became patroon of his own colony, which he called *Colen-Donck*.

POLITICS

From his base in Colen-Donck, van der Donck practiced law and involved himself in the life of the New Amsterdam colony. The Dutch West Indies Company had founded New Netherlands for commercial purposes rather than colonization and had therefore granted Kieft wide powers to regulate daily life. In the aftermath of Keift's ill-advised war, the traumatized Dutch settlers were in open conflict with the colony's director-general. The settlers, led by van der Donck, demanded sweeping administrative change. Van der

Donck was instrumental in having Kieft recalled. However, his petition for a representative-style government went unheeded. Kieft's successor, Peter Stuyvesant (*see entry on Stuyvesant*), initially sought to calm the situation by requesting that the Dutch citizens of New Amsterdam nominate eighteen representatives, from which pool he would create a nine-member advisory council. In 1649, Stuyvesant appointed van der Donck to be a member of this Council of Nine. The group in turn selected van der Donck to be their president. However, the Council of Nine almost immediately clashed with Stuyvesant over duties and fees claimed by the West Indies Company. Stuyvesant disbanded the council and accused van der Donck of "Encroachment on the Privileges of the Company."[305] Reconstituting the council with his own handpicked members, Stuyvesant had van der Donck declared a "rebel against justice," for which he was fined sixty guilders and enjoined from continuing his rebellious behaviors.[306]

But van der Donck had become a leader in voicing settler complaints against Stuyvesant. As a result, in 1649, van der Donck found himself subject to house arrest for the contents of his diary, which allegedly contained "calumnies and aspersions" in the form of allegedly slanderous accusations against Stuyvesant and his management of New Netherlands.[307] It took the intercession of the council to have van der Donck released.

Once he was freed, van der Donck sailed back to the Netherlands as part of a three-person delegation to try to persuade the Dutch governing body to form a representative government in New Netherlands. Their petition, *Remonstrances of New Netherland, Concerning Its Location, Frutifulness, and Sorry Condition*,[308] was published and widely circulated. This petition accused Stuyvesant of abusing his director role and "behaving not like a judge but like a zealous advocate" who "browbeat dispute[d] with and harass[ed] the colonists.[309] Throughout his time at The Hague, van der Donck received letters describing the conditions in New Netherlands in increasingly dire terms. These missives presciently predicted that unless Stuyvesant was removed, the increasingly dispirited colony was vulnerable to falling into foreign hands. The Dutch government initially granted the petition, awarding New Amsterdam a municipal charter and recalling Stuyvesant.[310] However, the Anglo-Dutch War, which began in 1652, prompted the Dutch government to reverse its decision to recall Stuyvesant.[311]

During the period he was stranded in the Dutch Republic, van der Donck wrote *Description of New Netherlands*. In this book, van der Donck painted New Netherlands as "a very beautiful, pleasant, healthy and delightful land, where all manner of men can more easily earn a good living and make their way in the world than in the Netherlands or any other part of the globe that I know."[312]

Van der Donck devoted thirty pages of this treatise to an ethnographic description of the lives of the Native peoples he had observed. His writing documented rich ethnographic details of Indian farming practices, clothing, family life, weapons, monetary systems and beliefs.[313] He obtained a fifteen-year copyright for the work from the Dutch government in 1653.[314]

Van der Donck died in 1655 or 1656, probably a victim of the Susquehannock attack on New Netherlands known as the Peach War. He was somewhere between thirty-five and thirty-seven.

FUN FACT Stuyvesant kept van der Donck stranded in the Netherlands for years by the simple expedient of refusing van der Donck passage on any West Indies Company ship.[*] It was only in 1653 that van der Donck was able to return to New Netherlands. Upon his return, his law practice was restricted. He was allowed to give advice but was denied the ability to represent clients in court.

---

* Petition of Adriaen van der Donck to the States General, in Fernow, supra note 339 at 476.

Chapter 4

JOHN JACKSON

THE GENTLEMAN FARMER

Jackson Heights was named after John Clews Jackson (April 2, 1809–September 18, 1889).

FAMILY BUSINESS

John Clews Jackson was born in Staffordshire, England, in 1809 to parents Mary Clews Jackson and William Jackson. His mother's family were wealthy pottery owners. He and his brother Job joined their uncles Ralph and James Clews in the family pottery business at a young age. Theirs was one of hundreds of potteries in North Staffordshire exporting porcelain and other pottery. America was by far the biggest customer for these wares.[315] In 1830, John and Job decided to start their own company. The next year, John traveled to America to begin securing customers using the Clews client list as a starting point. Outraged by this betrayal, the uncles wrote to their American customers warning that John did not represent them and claiming that "we are not afraid of them doing us harm as they are of no extent."[316] Jackson's arrival in New York was announced in the *New York Spectator*.[317]

John C. Jackson. *Originally published in* History of Queens County, with Illustrations, Portraits & Sketches of Prominent Families and Individuals *(1882)*.

Jackson Bros. bill of lading. *Used with permission from the Winterthur Library, Joseph Downs Collection of Manuscripts and Printed Ephemera.*

The Jackson brothers succeeded far beyond their uncles' predictions. In 1833, John moved permanently to America and established an importing business. He left Job to manage the pottery while he capitalized on their Staffordshire connections to meet a growing American demand for fine pottery. By 1834, the Jackson brothers were selling job lots of their pottery by the thousands. One of their platters is included in the Metropolitan Museum of Art's European Decorative Arts Collection.[318] However, worker struggles over poor wages and working conditions disrupted the Staffordshire pottery industry. By 1835, both the Clews and the Jackson pottery enterprises were bankrupt.[319]

Mired in debt, James Clews followed his nephews to America, where he started the Indiana pottery company in Troy, Indiana. By 1842, James had apparently rebuilt his wealth enough to sell out his share of the business and return to England with his family. John and Job Jackson, however, stayed in America and turned their talents exclusively to retail—becoming merchant dealers bridging the gap between the potteries of their native Staffordshire and the markets of New York. They established a very successful shop on Water Street. Little is known of Job, but at his death, John's fortune was valued at more than $1 million.[320]

In 1834, John married Martha Moore Riker, the daughter of Captain Andrew Riker (*see entry on Riker*) who was reputed to be the wealthiest heiress in the area.[321] They moved to Long Island City, where they had one daughter, Mary Ann Riker.

BUSINESS DEALINGS

Avidly interested in cattle breeding and agriculture, Jackson spent many years as president of the Queens County Agricultural Society and twice served as vice president of the New York State Agricultural Society. The society hosted an annual agricultural fair.

Jackson soon branched out from pottery, becoming a trustee of the Commercial Mutual Insurance Company, a director of the Flushing Railroad, a commissioner of the Central Railroad Company of Long Island and a founder of the Coal and Iron Exchange. In 1857, Jackson formed the Hunter's Point, Newtown and Flushing Turnpike Company to build a road connecting the Hunters Point ferry terminal with Flushing Bay. The road, which was completed in 1859, ran directly from Jackson's home in Long Island City to Flushing. Named Jackson Avenue in his honor, the road was originally built as a privately owned toll road.[322] In 1871, the New York legislature passed an act eliminating the tolls on Jackson Avenue while directing the towns of Flushing and Newtown to pay Jackson's turnpike company $70,000 in compensation (roughly $1.8 million in 2022 dollars).[323] A section of this road continues to bear Jackson's name, but most of the road is now called Northern Boulevard.

JACKSON HEIGHTS

Jackson died on September 18, 1889, while plans were being made to build the Queensboro Bridge to connect Manhattan with Long Island City at Jackson Avenue. It took another twenty years for the bridge to be built, and when it opened in June 1909, the Queensboro Bridge was the longest cantilevered structure in the world. The new bridge had two elevated railway lines, two trolley lines, six carriage lanes and two pedestrian walkways.

The bridge sparked a real estate boom in what had been a sparsely populated area of

FUN FACT The competitions at the fair included livestock, vegetables and craftwork. Among the categories were "best trotter in harness driven by the owner" and "best butter made by a girl under 21."* While many of the prizes were just a few dollars, the prize for best stallion could range from $25 to $100 (about $920 to $3,700 today). Jackson first participated in the 1852 Queens Agricultural Fair, where he won prizes in every category he entered. Martha Jackson often served as a judge for the "Ladies' Competitions."†

---

* W.W Munsell History of Queens County, with Illustrations, Portraits & Sketches of Prominent Families, and Individuals 64, 269–70 (1882).
† Local Intelligence: Queens County Agricultural Fair, N.Y. Times (Sept. 21, 1862).

Queensboro Bridge. *Library of Congress.*

Queens, with the area population doubling virtually overnight. One of the first developments was named Jackson Heights in Jackson's honor. Taking inspiration from British architect Ebenezer Howard's Garden City model, Jackson Heights was a planned low-density community with the first garden apartments and cooperative apartments in the United States. Indeed, the term "garden apartment" comes from the first Jackson Heights building, which was named Garden Apartments. These homes targeted middle- and upper-income Manhattanites looking for a green environment for their families. To that end, the apartments were built around shared garden spaces and included relatively high-end features like fireplaces, ornate exteriors, bathtubs and beautiful wood floors.

Advertisements for the development made it clear that only white, Anglo-Saxon Protestants were welcome, and the deeds were restricted to explicitly exclude Jews, Catholics and Blacks. When the United States Supreme Court ruled these deed restrictions unconstitutional,[324] this de jure segregation began to break down. Jews and Catholics began moving into Jackson Heights almost immediately. However, active discrimination prevented Black families from moving into the neighborhood until the Fair Housing Act became law in the late 1960s. Today's Jackson Heights is one of the most diverse communities in the world.

FUN FACT In April 1929, the Prudential Insurance Company agreed to issue twenty-year mortgages for the purchase of these Jackson Heights apartments. These were the longest mortgages ever financed, and the *New York Times* predicted that they would set a new standard for long-term mortgage loans.

Chapter 5

THE LENOXES

THE ARDENT FEDERALIST (ROBERT) AND THE BOOK COLLECTOR (JAMES)

Lennox Hill is named after Robert Lenox (1759–1839), a Scottish immigrant to New York who was one of the wealthiest merchants of his day. Lenox Avenue is named after his son James Lenox (1800–1880), an art and book collector who donated millions to charities in the City.

FAMILY LIFE

On December 31, 1759, Robert Lenox was born in Kirkcudbright, Scotland, to parents James Lenox and Elizabeth (Sproat) Lenox. He was one of eleven children. Along with his brothers David and William, Robert Lenox immigrated to America just prior to the Revolution. There the brothers joined their uncle David Sproat and helped him build a family mercantile business.

During the Revolutionary War, the family's loyalties were divided. David Sproat and William Lenox joining the British (serving as commissaries general of prisoners for the navy and army, respectively), while David Lenox

Robert Lenox, portrait by James Trumbull. *Courtesy of New York Public Library.*

became a major in the Continental army. Robert did not join either side of the conflict. Instead, he looked after the family business, traveling extensively to the West Indies and Charleston. At one point, he was taken prisoner by a French man-o'-war, but his brother David intervened to secure his release.

After the war, Robert Lenox married Rachel Carmer. Together, they had twelve children, including James Lenox (*see below*). James was the only son to survive to adulthood, along with five of his sisters.

BUSINESS

In 1796, Robert and his brother James established the commercial house of Lenox and Maitland with William Maitland. Their ships crisscrossed the Atlantic. Although Lenox and Maitland ships did not directly participate in the slave trade by carrying enslaved people, they did carry goods like rum and sugar produced by those enslaved in the West Indies. The firm of Lenox and Maitland thus formed a vital link in the slavery economy by connecting plantations in Jamaica and Cuba with markets in New York and Europe.[325] Moreover, Robert personally participated in slavery—the 1800 census reported four enslaved persons in his household. In 1817, Robert advertised a sizable reward for the return of Abraham Sherrit, a young Black man whom the ad characterized as an escaped slave.[326]

During the War of 1812, Lenox and Maitland also benefited from privateer activities—selling goods seized from ships flying "enemy" flags. When their own cargos or ships were seized, they litigated for compensation, bringing multiple such cases before the Supreme Court. Overall, it was an astonishingly lucrative business. Robert became one of the most influential businessmen in New York. Indeed, for many years, he was the most successful merchant in the country.[327] His wealth was rivaled only by that of John Jacob Astor (*see entry on Astor*).

Politically, Robert Lenox was an ardent Federalist and a strong advocate of free trade. He was twice elected an alderman of New York City: from 1795 to 1797 and from 1800 to 1802. Early in his first term, Robert stumbled into controversy. He helped convict two Irish immigrants on trumped-up charges after they reputedly insulted a fellow alderman named Gabriel Furman. The case inflamed anti-Federalist sentiment and resulted in

FUN FACT David Sproat was friends with fellow Scotsman and founder of the United States Navy John Paul Jones. Before the Revolution, Sprout acted as Jones's Philadelphia agent.

an anonymous broadside impugning Robert's patriotism by accusing him of "embitter[ing] the miseries of the unfortunate American prisoners" on the HMS *Jersey* who refused to join the British army during the occupation of New York.[328] Since Robert's uncle David Sproat had been reviled for his role in overseeing those same prisoners, the charges stuck.[329] A few days later, the paper published Robert's response,[330] but his reputation took a hit. When the allegations resurfaced in 1802, Robert produced numerous testimonials, including one from Alexander Hamilton, vouching for Robert's "kind and accommodating disposition toward our prisoners" during the British occupation of New York.[331]

Robert Lenox was active in New York City's civic affairs. He was president of the St. Andrews Society from 1798 to 1813. Along with Archibald Gracie and Alexander Hamilton, Robert helped found New York City's first maternity hospital, the Lying-in Hospital, in 1799. Robert was the largest donor and served as the hospital's president from 1829 to 1835. He also served as president of the New York Chamber of Commerce for more than a decade and was chair of the board of managers of the Sailor's Snug Harbor, a trustee of Princeton College and an elder and major benefactor of the First Presbyterian Church.[332]

James Lenox: The Book Collector

James Lenox, portrait by Sir Francis Grant. *Courtesy of New York Public Library.*

Robert's son James Lenox was born on August 19, 1800. James was educated at Princeton Seminary before studying law at Columbia University and becoming a member of the bar. In 1839, when Robert Lenox died at age eighty-one, James inherited an enormous fortune. Indeed, in the 1860s, James was the third-richest man in New York City.

His inheritance included roughly thirty acres between 4th and 5th Avenues, bounded by 68th and 74th Streets, an area then known as Lenox Farm. In his will, Robert advised James to hold on to this property, as he (Robert) predicted it would become much more valuable as "a village" grew up around it. James followed his father's prescient advice and held onto the land

---

* Realty Romance in Old Lenox Farm, N.Y. Times (Dec. 15, 1918).

for decades. This land is now known as Lenox Hill—one of New York City's ritzier neighborhoods.

The parcel that Robert held included 198 lots, for which he paid roughly $2.23 per lot. Fifty years later, James sold those lots for $5,575 each.[333] By 1874, each lot was worth $30,000. The land sales netted James over $3 million (more than $60 million today). James also donated parcels worth nearly another $3 million to various charities.[334] James and his sister Henrietta lived together in their family home on Lenox Farm until their deaths.

BOOKS AND ART

James Lenox was a reclusive man who never married and died without children. His *New York Times* obituary turned this into a positive, eulogizing Lenox by noting that "his blameless life is secure from unworthy reflection in the lives of dissolute or unmanly sons. There will be no strife over his grave."[335] The *Times* had little else to work with, as on his deathbed, James Lenox had specifically requested that "the private particulars of his life might not be publicly canvassed."[336]

For most of his life, James Lenox devoted himself to collecting rare books and art. He frequently made generous contributions to various New York cultural institutions. In 1859, for example, he donated thirteen so-called Nineveh marbles to the New York Historical Society. These carvings had been taken from the Sardanapalus Temple in Assyria and were one of just two such sets of relics in existence; the other was housed at the British Museum.[337] Today, these marbles are in the Brooklyn Museum.

Lenox's book collection occupied most of his time and energy. The collection boasted the first Gutenberg

---

* Testimonial to Commodore Perry, N.Y. Times (Jan. 18, 1855).

Bible in the Americas and an unrivaled collection of early Americana, including one of two original copies of Adriaen van der Donck's *Description of New Netherland* (*see entry on van der Donck*). Overall, Lenox's collection was reputed to be the most expensive and extensive private collection in the Western Hemisphere.

In 1870, an act of the New York state legislature incorporated the Lenox Library. Lenox then donated land and money to build a home for his collection. Lenox hired Richard Morris Hunt, American architecture's "first and greatest statesman,"[338] to build the Lenox Library. With a prime 5th Avenue location overlooking Central Park, the Beaux Arts–style library he designed was reputedly an architectural gem. Indeed, when the Municipal Arts Society erected a memorial to Richard Morris Hunt in 1898, the spot they selected was in front of the Lenox Library.

Admission to the Lenox Library was by ticket, with admission cards mailed to those who requested them. In its first year, fifteen thousand people visited the Lenox Library. For its first decade, the Lenox Library only displayed material and did not allow visitors physical access to the collection.

Lenox Avenue/Malcom X Boulevard and 125th Street. *Photo by Rebecca Bratspies.*

In 1895, the Lenox Library combined with the Astor Library (*see entry on Astor*) to become the New York Public Library. After the main New York Public Library was built on Bryant Square (*see entry on Bryant*), the Lenox Collection was moved there.[339] Almost immediately, the library sold the Lenox Library building to Henry Clay Frick. Frick proceeded to dismantle the building to build his mansion, which now houses the Frick Collection.

Lenox was also a founder and major benefactor of the Presbyterian Hospital (now Columbia-Presbyterian), as well as the Presbyterian Home for Aged Women (now known as the James Lenox House).

FUN FACT To commemorate the founding of the New York City Library, literary critic Laurence Hutton wrote an essay in *Harper's Weekly* intending to praise Lenox's "vast bequests" to New York City. A typographic error instead had him praising Lenox's "vest buttons."*

* Laurence Hutton, Typographical Errors, Tucamacari News (October 13, 1906).

He was a trustee of the College of New Jersey (now Princeton University) and a trustee, director and major donor to the Princeton Seminary.

Lenox died in 1890, and in 1897, 6th Avenue above 110th Street was renamed in his honor. The primary north–south route through Harlem, Lenox Avenue was inextricably associated with the 1930s Harlem Renaissance. Indeed, Langston Hughes once described Lenox Avenue as "Harlem's Heartbeat." To honor this heritage, Lenox Avenue was co-named Malcom X Boulevard in 1987. The street officially bears both names but is more often referred to as Malcom X Boulevard.

Chapter 6

PETER STUYVESANT

THE LAST DUTCH DIRECTOR-GENERAL

S tuyvesant Town, the neighborhood of Bedford-Stuyvesant and
Stuyvesant High School are all named after Peter (Petrus) Stuyvesant,
the last Dutch director-general of the colony of New Netherlands.
Peter Stuyvesant was born in approximately 1612 in the Netherlands.
He studied philosophy at the University of Franeker but was expelled for
seducing his landlord's daughter. After being caught, Stuyvesant began his
career with the Dutch West Indies Company. He served as director of the
colony of Curaçao from 1642 to 1644. During an attack on the island of

Peter Stuyvesant, painted by
Frédéric. *Courtesy of the New York
Public Library.*

St. Maarten, Stuyvesant lost his right leg in
a skirmish with Spanish forces. He spent the
rest of his life with a peg leg. The wounded
Stuyvesant returned to Leiden to convalesce
with his sister Anna. There he met Judith
Bayard, sister to Anna's husband, Samuel
Bayard. The two were married in 1645, and
together they had two sons, Nicholas and
Balthazar.

The Dutch West Indies Company
selected the newly married Stuyvesant to
head the New Netherlands Colony. Arriving
in the city of New Amsterdam in 1647,
Stuyvesant's first official act was to ban
the sale of alcohol after 8:00 p.m. (and

on Sundays before 2:00 p.m.).[340] His volatile temperament led him into constant conflict with those he was charged with managing. He quarreled with leading Dutch settlers and maintained vindictive feuds with those he considered political enemies.[341]

Adriaen van der Donck (*see entry on van der Donck*) emerged as a leader of the resistance to Stuyvesant's autocratic rule. In 1649, van der Donck headed a delegation that traveled to Holland to try to get Stuyvesant removed from office.[342] The Dutch government initially agreed to recall Stuyvesant.[343] However, upon the outbreak of the 1652 Anglo-Dutch War, the Dutch government opted to leave Stuyvesant in place.[344] In all, Stuyvesant spent seventeen years as director-general of New Netherlands.

Contrary to the general atmosphere of religious tolerance prevalent in the Dutch states, Stuyvesant opposed religious freedom in New Netherlands. In 1656, he banned all religious practices outside the Dutch Reformed Church. In particular, Jews, Quakers, Lutherans and Catholics found it difficult to immigrate to or worship freely in Stuyvesant's New Netherlands. Stuyvesant specifically tried to expel the colony's Jews, charged them special taxes and denied them permits. He also refused to allow them to open a synagogue.

A 1957 U.S. postage stamp commemorating religious freedom and the *Flushing Remonstrance* of 1657. *Wikimedia Commons.*

FUN FACT In 1657, thirty English residents of Flushing sent Stuyvesant a petition that became known as the *Flushing Remonstrance*. In it, the residents opposed Styuvesant's ban on Quaker worship and urged freedom of religion more generally. After being arrested for allowing a Quaker meeting in his house, John Bowne traveled to Holland and persuaded the Dutch West Indies Company to rescind Stuyvesant's draconian law. The company directed Stuyvesant to "allow every one to have his own belief as long as he behaved quietly and legally, gave no offence to his neighbors, and did not oppose the government."* In 1957, the U.S. Post Office issued a three-cent stamp commemorating the 300th anniversary of the *Flushing Remonstrance*.

---

* Michael Kammen, Colonial New York: A History 62 (1975).

Stuyvesant also actively supported the slave trade. In 1660, Stuyvesant supervised the first slave auction of human beings in the colony—a practice that continued throughout his directorship. He not only facilitated importing enslaved Africans into the colony but also was the largest slaveholder in the colony, personally enslaving 40 Africans. In 1664, one of Stuyvesant's last acts was to supervise the arrival of the slave ship *Gideon*, which at Stuyvesant's behest brought 290 captured African men and women into the colony, thereby doubling New Amsterdam's enslaved population.[345]

In August 1664, four British warships under the command of Richard Nicolls sailed into the Hudson Bay and claimed New Amsterdam in the name of the Duke of York (later King James II). Even though the Dutch were vastly outnumbered and their defensive position was hopeless, Stuyvesant initially refused to surrender, announcing that "he would rather be carried a corpse to his grave." However, New Amsterdam's disaffected citizens did not rally around him. Trapped between the English forces and his own settlers who advocated surrender, Stuyvesant could not hold out long. On September 8, 1664, Stuyvesant signed articles of capitulation, ceding New Amsterdam to Nicolls, who promptly renamed the colony New York and raised the English flag over the newly renamed Fort James. In 1665, Nicolls appointed Thomas Willetts mayor of New York.

Stuyvesant spent the remainder of his life on his sixty-two-acre farm, or *bouwerie*, located in today's East Village and Stuyvesant Town. The Bowery takes its name from the Dutch word for farm. His house was destroyed by a fire in 1777.

Stuyvesant died in August 1672. He was eighty years old. His body was entombed in a vault in St. Mark's Church in the Bowery. The stone covering his tomb reads, "In this vault lies buried Petrus Stuyvesant late Captain General and Governor in Chief of Amsterdam in New Netherland now called New York and the Dutch West Indies Islands. Died February A.D. 1672."

Stuyvesant Town–Peter Cooper Village

Stuyvesant Town–Peter Cooper Village is a 11,500-unit residential complex in lower Manhattan. It was built through a collaboration between the City, led by Parks Commissioner Robert Moses, and a private developer, the Metropolitan Life Company. To get the land, Moses declared the entire existing neighborhood, known as Gas House District, to be a slum and used eminent domain to raze eighteen city blocks. Thousands of people were

Stuyvesant Farm, from the *Plan of the City of New York in North America* by Ratzer, 1770. *Wikimedia Commons.*

evicted in what the *New York Times* called "the greatest and most significant mass movement of families in New York's history."[346] The result was seventy-two vacant acres that were turned over to Met Life to build Stuyvesant Town and Peter Cooper Village pursuant to a redevelopment contract with the City.

The complex's 1943 offering plan, which was approved by the City Board of Estimates, included a restrictive covenant banning Black people from renting the new apartments. Robert Moses vocally defended this racial discrimination as a legitimate exercise of the landlord's right to select tenants. A group of Black veterans who had been denied apartments under the racist policy sued. They were joined by white Stuyvesant and Peter Cooper residents who organized as the Town and Village Committee to End Discrimination in Stuyvesant Town. Thurgood Marshall represented the plaintiffs challenging the racially restrictive covenants. Samuel Seabury represented Stuyvesant Town to defend the restrictive covenants.

In 1949, the New York Court of Appeals ruled that the state constitution's guarantee of equal protection did not apply to Metropolitan, leaving the company free to discriminate against Black tenants.[347] Outrage was swift. City councilmember Stanley Isaacs introduced legislation to bar discrimination at the development. Before the legislation was enacted, however, social and political pressure forced Met Life to reverse course. In 1950, the company announced that it would begin renting to "qualified" Black applicants.[348] However, the residents who had challenged the racially discriminatory policies were denied lease renewals and were forced out of the complex.[349]

In 2005, real estate investing firm Tishman Speyer purchased Stuyvesant Town and Peter Cooper Village from Met Life for $5.4 billion. The new owners' plan to pay for this purchase involved taking most of the apartments out of rent stabilization and jacking up rents.[350] The New York Court of Appeals found this unlawful. The court put thousands of apartments back into rent stabilization, requiring Tishman Speyer to refund rent overcharges.[351] In 2009, Tishman Speyer defaulted on its mortgage and surrendered Stuyvesant Town to its lenders.

Stuyvesant High School is New York City's most famous specialized high school. Admission to the school is highly coveted, as it consistently ranks as one of the best schools in the country. Students are selected based entirely on a single test taken by eighth-grade students, and the school has come under fire because so few Black and Latinx students are offered admission. Located just blocks from the Twin Towers, Stuyvesant was evacuated on 9/11. Many students suffer from lingering health effects from exposure to the toxic environment after the catastrophe.

Chapter 7

CHARLES A. WILLETS

ACCIDENTAL FAME

Willets Point is a peninsula in Queens named after landowner and nurseryman Charles Augustus Willets (1781–1833). Willets Point is the site of Fort Totten and is the designation of the seven-train subway stop for Citi Fields, where the Mets play. The stop was formerly the Willets Point–Shea Stadium stop (*see entry on Shea*).

A common error is to assume that Willets Point was named after Thomas Willett, the first (and third) mayor of New York, who took office after the British captured New Amsterdam from the Dutch in 1665. Willett served two one-year terms as mayor, from 1665 to 1666 and 1667 to 1668. However, Willets Point peninsula was actually named after Charles and Ann Willets, who purchased the land in 1829 and ran the first local nursery there.

Charles and Ann were married in about 1822 and had three children: Martha, Charles and Mary.[352] The Willetses' Greek Revival–style house still stands on the grounds of Fort Totten, though it is increasingly derelict.[353] The Willetses purchased the peninsula from Jacob Wilkins,[354] a descendant of the Thorne family whose interest in the land dated back to a 1645 grant from New Netherlands director-general Kieft. In the deed of sale, Wilkins reserved the portion of the land that served as a family cemetery, as well as a right-of-way to access the cemetery.[355] As late as 1898, there was official recognition of the existence of the cemetery and the validity of Wilkins's right-of-way. However, over time, the location of the cemetery was lost, and Wilkins's distant descendants are still trying (unsuccessfully) to assert their rights.[356]

Mets–Willets Point subway stop. *Photo by DanTD, Wikimedia Commons.*

Willets's gravestone. *Photo by Jeffrey Bratspies.*

Charles Willets died in April 1833. His grave marker—which still stands at Fort Totten even though he was reburied with his family in Green Wood Cemetery—incorrectly records his death as 1832. Ann remarried and lived until 1890.

After Charles's death, the land passed to his son, also named Charles A. Willets. He held onto the land until 1852, when he sold approximately 152 acres to one Frederick Wissmann for $35,500 (approximately $223 per acre).[357]

A few years later, the federal government decided to purchase land in the area to build a fort "opposite Fort Schuyler" on the Throgs Neck of Long Island. Brigadier General Joseph G. Totten, chief of the army's Engineering Division, was put in charge of acquiring the land. Totten identified Willets Point as the most appropriate site. However, the purchase of Willets Point became a major corruption scandal implicating military and civilian officials.

Wissmann had sold some of his Willets Point land in 1856 for $500 per acre. Yet the very next year, he demanded $1,000 per acre from the government—for a total of $130,000.[358] Thinking this price too high, General Totten sought authorization to use eminent domain to condemn the land.

FUN FACT William Thorne Sr., the original patent holder, was one of the Dutch colonists who signed the *Flushing Remonstrance* to Peter Stuyvesant.[*]

---

* Nir, supra note 396.

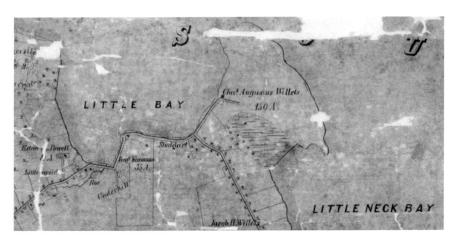

An 1852 map of Kings and part of Queens Counties engraved by Korff brothers and originally published by Dripps. *Library of Congress.*

While the government pursued condemnation authorization, a group of speculators obtained an option on the property for $130,000.[359] Their option was contingent on the government purchasing Willets Point for $200,000. These speculators then offered the land directly to Secretary of War John B. Floyd. Secretary Floyd agreed to the price and authorized the purchase.

FUN FACT The original plans for a fortification at Willets Point were drawn up by Robert E. Lee at the behest of Congress. Yet it was fears of a Confederate attack on New York after the outbreak of the Civil War that spurred the work to fortify Willets Point.

Citing the "exorbitant and unjust price," the House of Representatives immediately launched an investigation into the facts and circumstances of this transaction.[360] Through this investigation, it became clear that the speculators were acting with the collusion of many of the government officials charged with overseeing the purchase, up to and including Secretary of War Floyd. One whistleblower complained, "I am not disposed to have speculations made upon the treasury for the aggrandizement of persons who deem it fair enough to cheat Uncle Sam if the opportunity offers."[361]

The United States began building the Willets Point fort to defend New York Harbor during the Civil War. However, advances in weaponry made stone forts obsolete, and the fort was never completed. Instead, General Sherman advocated using Willets Point for a new officer training school in engineering and torpedo mining. Thus, Willets Point became the training base for the U.S. Army Corps of Engineers. In 1898, President McKinley named the fortress Fort Totten to honor General Totten.[362]

During World War I, the first unit of the American Expeditionary Force to land in France came through Fort Totten.[363] Fort Totten housed the first

FUN FACT Secretary of War John B. Floyd was a Virginian, a slaveholder and an ardent supporter of slavery. As President Buchanan's secretary of war, he abused his position to funnel military supplies to the South in anticipation of the Civil War. Ulysses S. Grant accused him of "scatter[ing] the army" and "distribut[ing] the cannon and small arms from Northern arsenals throughout the South so as to be on hand when treason wanted them."*

After Lincoln was elected president, Floyd resigned as secretary of war for the United States of America. Within months, he was a general in the Confederate army. However, Floyd was so incompetent that Jefferson Davis relieved him of command in March 1862.

---

* Memoirs of General U.S. Grant, Chapter XVI.

FUN FACT In the mid-1870s, Dr. Walter Reed became post surgeon at Willets Point. It was there that he began studies into advances in military medicine.

radar station on the East Coast and remained a defense installation until the end of World War II. The fort was decommissioned in 1967. Today, Fort Totten is a park owned by the City of New York

The Willets Point neighborhood of Queens is not actually at Willets Point. Instead, the sixty-two-acre triangular tract straddles Corona and Flushing. It is wedged between the Van Wyck Expressway (*see entry on Van Wyck*) and Citi Field (*see entry on Shea*). Known locally as the Iron Triangle, Willets Point is one of the few remaining places in New York City with no sidewalks, no sewers and no streetlights.[364]

The development (or lack thereof) of Willets Point was one of Robert Moses's greatest defeats. During his term as president of the 1964 World's Fair, Moses tried to condemn property in Willets Point and expand Flushing Meadows Park. Local business owners opposed to the plan hired Mario Cuomo, then a young lawyer, to represent them. Cuomo's win eventually catapulted him into the governor's office.

In 2007, then-mayor Michael Bloomberg unveiled a plan to redevelop Willets Point from a flood-prone "eyesore and disgrace"[365] into New York's "first truly green community"[366] of apartments, office buildings, stores, restaurants and hotels. To that end, the City evicted most of the businesses. However, the plan was widely criticized as serving the needs of private developers rather than the public and was ultimately blocked by the courts. The area remains in limbo. The 2019 documentary *The Iron Triangle* tells the story of Willets Point as the front line of deindustrialization, urban renewal and gentrification.[367]

FUN FACT F. Scott Fitzgerald set key parts of *The Great Gatsby* in the neighborhood of Willets Point, which he renamed the Valley of Ash: "a fantastic farm where ashes grow like wheat into ridges and hills and grotesque gardens."*

* F. Scott Fitzgerald, The Great Gatsby 16 (1925); see also, Levi Asher, In Gatsby's Tracks: Locating the Valley of Ashes in a 1924 Photo, LiteraryKicks.com (Feb. 25, 2010).

PART V

INSTITUTIONS AND LANDMARKS

Chapter 1

GERTRUDE WHITNEY

THE REBEL HEIRESS

The Whitney Museum of Art is named after its founder and patron, sculptor Gertrude Vanderbilt Whitney (1875–1942).

FAMILY LIFE

Gertrude Vanderbilt Whitney. *Wikimedia Commons.*

Gertrude Vanderbilt Whitney was born on January 9, 1875, to parents Cornelius Vanderbilt II and Alice Claypoole Gwynne. As "the eldest daughter of the eldest son of the richest family in America"[368] and great-granddaughter of railroad baron "Commodore" Cornelius Vanderbilt, she lived a life of wealth and privilege. Whitney spent her summers at The Breakers and attended the exclusive Brearley School in Manhattan.

In 1860, Whitney married wealthy playboy Harry Payne Whitney. Together, they had three children and eight grandchildren. Despite having very little in common, their marriage lasted until his death in 1930. He left Whitney an estate of more than $72 million.

Art Career

A talented artist, Whitney broke out of the high society mode to study sculpture at a time when few women were accepted in the field. Neither her wealthy family nor her horse-obsessed husband supported her artistic aspirations. Nevertheless, Whitney studied first in New York City at the Art Students League of New York and later in Paris, where her work caught the eye of Auguste Rodin.[369] Concerned that her famous name would tag her as a dilettante, she originally worked under a pseudonym.

In 1907, Whitney bought a former hayloft in MacDougal Alley in Greenwich Village to build her studio. Outraged newspaper headlines blared, "Daughter of Cornelius Vanderbilt Will Live in Dingy New York Alley."[370] Despite the public scandal, Whitney made her MacDougal property into her studio and apparently lived the riotous bohemian lifestyle there—a sharp contrast to her otherwise aristocratic uptown existence. Over time, Whitney purchased the entire block and expanded her studio, turning it into the Whitney Studio club, a central gathering place for American artists and ultimately the first home of the Whitney Museum. Designated a National Historic Landmark in 1992 and a National Treasure in 2014, Whitney's studio is part of the New York Studio School, which has been struggling to maintain and restore it.

During World War I, Whitney was deeply involved with various relief efforts. For example, she personally funded construction of a 225-bed fully operational hospital in Juilly, France, close to the front lines, and recruited its medical staff. She also donated an entire mobile field unit to the American Field Service. Whitney made multiple visits to the war zone. She frequently sketched the patients at the facilities her wealth had funded.

FUN FACT Whitney had a youthful romance with Esther Hunt, daughter of architect Richard Morris Hunt (architect of the Lenox Library). Whitney described it as one of the "thrills of my life when Esther kissed me." Her disapproving family forbade her to see Esther.

After the war, Whitney translated those wartime experiences into her art. She sculpted the Washington Heights War Memorial at 168th Street and Broadway; panels for the New York victory arch; and a statue in St. Nazaire, France, where the first contingent of the American Expeditionary Force landed. She also designed a massive cubist Columbus statue in Huelva, Spain. This statute towers 114 feet over the harbor that launched Columbus's 1492 voyage. She viewed these statues as "links which will serve to bind Europe

Gertrude Vanderbilt Whitney. *Library of Congress.*

and the United States even closer."[371] Her last sculptures were a monument to Peter Stuyvesant and *To the Morrow* or *The Spirit of Flight*, commissioned for the 1939 World's Fair in Flushing Meadow.

Whitney's best work is generally considered to be her design for the 1922 *Titanic* memorial. Whitney's design for the statue was selected through a

FUN FACT Whitney's dramatic statue of a partially clothed young man standing with arms spread wide was likely the inspiration for an iconic scene in the 1997 *Titanic* movie.

Gertrude Whitney's *Titanic* memorial. *Wikimedia Commons.*

competition restricted to female artists,[372] and she received a commission of $43,000 (roughly $1.12 million today).

The *Titanic* memorial design was approved by the U.S. Commission on Fine Arts in 1919. However, it took another decade to settle on a location. After much wrangling, Congress finally approved a location, and former first lady Helen Taft unveiled the statue in 1931. However, during the construction of the Kennedy Center, the statue was evicted and relocated to a waterfront park near Fort McNair in Southwest Washington, D.C.

The Women's Titanic Memorial Committee raised funds for the statue by soliciting small (one- and five-dollar) donations from women across America. The statue is dedicated "to the brave men who perished in the *Titanic* April 15, 1912. They gave their lives that women and children might be saved." (Of course, scores of children and women also died in the wreck, mostly third-class passengers.) Whitney had a very personal stake in this project—for her, it commemorated not only those who died in the 1912 *Titanic* disaster but also her brother Alfred, who died in similar circumstances with the 1915 sinking of the *Lusitania*. During his life, Alfred had been an extravagant playboy, but in the moment of crisis, he reportedly stepped up, organizing lifeboat evacuations and giving his own life vest to a second-class female passenger with a baby.

Whitney's work received critical acclaim in both Europe and the United States. She had solo shows in London and Paris and organized an Overseas Exhibition of American Art. Throughout her career, Whitney leveraged both her artistic prestige and her wealth to support and expand roles for female artists in a profession that routinely excluded or diminished them.

She supported and exhibited in women-only shows and demanded that women be included in mixed shows.

Whitney championed contemporary American art at a time when American museums and collectors largely limited themselves to "real" (meaning European) art. In 1918, she opened the Whitney Studio club to create opportunities for New York artists to socialize, share ideas and exhibit their work. At its peak, the club had over four hundred members. Whitney frequently provided housing and stipends to promising club members. She actively bought from new artists, amassing an enormous collection of modern American works. In 1929, she tried to donate this collection to the New York Metropolitan Museum of Art. However, her donation was rejected (along with the funds to build a wing to display the art) because the museum "did not take American art." In response, Whitney decided to build her own museum. She transformed the Whitney Club into the Whitney Studio Galleries and, in 1931, into the Whitney Museum of American Art.

Whitney's work won her significant recognition. She was awarded honorary doctorates by Russell Sage (doctor of human letters) and Rutgers (doctorate of art)[373] and honorary master's degrees from Tufts and NYU. The president of France named Whitney a chevalier of the French Legion of Honor in 1926.[374] Among the more interesting awards given to Whitney, she was named to the National Dairy Association National Honor Roll in 1941 for developing a herd of fourteen cows that produced 427 pounds of butter.[375]

GLORIA VANDERBILT CUSTODY BATTLE

In 1934, Whitney was involved in a high-profile custody battle over her ten-year-old niece Gloria Vanderbilt (yes, the jeans one). The custody battle was really a fight over money. Young Gloria's father had died two years earlier, leaving his daughter heir to millions held in trust. Her mother, also named Gloria, used the interest from the trust to fund a lavish life, which included affairs with Lady Milford-Haven and an engagement to Prince Gottfried of Hohenlohe-Langenburg. Barely more than a child herself, Gloria Sr. apparently showed little maternal interest in young Gloria.

When young Gloria needed a tonsillectomy, she recuperated with Whitney. Two years later, young Gloria was still living with Whitney, who had enrolled her in school and was signing her report cards. Her mother had disappeared—rushing back to a glamourous whirlwind life in

Europe. But without her child, Gloria Sr.'s allowance from the trust was in jeopardy.[376] She came back to New York and filed a petition for custody. (Because Gloria Sr. was still a minor herself, she needed court intervention to reclaim her child.)

The trial was a media circus. Weeks of salacious testimony shredded Gloria Sr.'s character, morals and lifestyle. The judge awarded primary custody to Whitney, finding Gloria Sr.'s lifestyle "in every way unsuitable, unfit, improper" for raising a child.[377] Gloria Sr. got weekend visits and a month in the summer. The $4,000 per month income from the trust (roughly $81,000 in today's dollars) was divided accordingly. In the 1980s, a bestselling book titled *Little Gloria...Happy at Last* and a TV miniseries starting Angela Lansbury and Bette Davis rehashed this sensational custody battle. Gloria Vanderbilt herself wrote about the custody saga in *Nothing Left Unsaid*, a memoir she coauthored with her son, Anderson Cooper.

Whitney died in New York City on April 18, 1942, at the age of sixty-seven. In her will, she left the Whitney Museum $2.5 million. The Whitney Museum held a memorial exhibition honoring her in early 1943.

Chapter 2

THE RIKERS

THE YANKEE PRIVATEER (ANDREW) AND THE KIDNAPPING CLUB MEMBER (RICHARD)

Rikers Island is part of the traditional territory of the Munsee Lenape, Wappinger and Matinecock tribes.[378] In 1638, nineteen-year-old Abraham Rycken received a New Netherlands land grant from Dutch West Indies director-general Willem Kieft. Rycken, who was from an aristocratic Lower Saxony family, is assumed to have immigrated soon after. In 1654, Peter Stuyvesant (*see entry on Stuyvesant*) granted Rycken another large tract in Newtown (present-day Long Island City and Astoria). In 1664, Ryken added to his landholdings by acquiring what is now known as Rikers Island by patent deed from Stuyvesant just before the Dutch colony surrendered to England.[379] In 1677, the British ratified Rycken's ownership of the island under the patent from Stuyvesant. The house that Abraham Rycken built is still standing and occupied in Astoria Queens. It is the oldest private dwelling in New York City.

The Rycken family were slaveholders who used the labor of enslaved people to build their fortune.[380] They then parlayed this wealth into social prominence. The family anglicized its name to Riker in the mid-1700s.

ANDREW RIKER

The island gets its name from the exploits of Captain Andrew Riker (September 21, 1771–October 17, 1817), an important naval figure from the War of 1812. Andrew was the middle son of Samuel Riker and Anna

Laurence and great-grandson of Abraham Rycken. One of twelve children, Andrew grew up in a prosperous Revolutionary household. Riker's father, Samuel, was a strong advocate of independence, serving as a lieutenant in the Light Horse Regiment of the Continental army. After the war, Samuel Riker was twice elected to represent New York's First Congressional District.[381]

Andrew Riker was a sailor initially involved in the East India trade. After he was rated as ships' master, Riker sailed the *Eagle*, which brought Irish immigrants to the United States. In 1802, he married Margaret Moore. Together, they had seven children, all of whom lived to adulthood.

Andrew Riker. *Photo of Tiffany Studio portrait, courtesy of Isobel Ellis.*

During the War of 1812, Riker sailed the booby-trapped *Eagle* to Waterford, Connecticut, as part of a plot to destroy the HMS *Ramillies*—the seventy-four-gun flagship of the British fleet blockading Long Island Sound. The idea was to pack the *Eagle* with gunpowder and then maneuver it close to the British fleet and ignite the explosives. The attempt failed to destroy the British ship but did kill eleven of the British soldiers who had boarded the *Eagle*.

During the War of 1812, the United States supplemented its meager navy with privateers—privately owned merchant ships armed by their owners and sent out to capture merchant ships flying the enemy's flag. The only thing differentiating privateers from pirates was that privateers held a letter of marque, a license from the government to attack and capture enemy ships and then to sell those captured ships and their cargo for profit. In 1813, Riker built and outfitted two privateers, the *Saratoga* and the *Yorktown*, and obtained a letter of marque allowing him to take British vessels. He sold subscription

FUN FACT Andrew and Margaret Riker lived in Oak Hill, a house located in Long Island City. The property ultimately devolved to their daughter Martha, who lived there with her spouse, John Clews Jackson (*see entry on Jackson*). In 1910, Oak Hill was moved to an estate in New Jersey, and the land on which it stood was repurposed as the site of William Cullen Bryant High School (*see entry on Bryant*).*

---

* Edgar Allen Nutt, The Rikers: Their Island, Homes, Cemetery and Early Genealogy (2004).

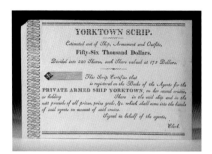

Andrew Riker privateer subscription.
Courtesy of Back Creek Books and Rockford E. Toews.

shares for each voyage, with investors contributing $175 per share in exchange for a share of the prizes that would "come into the hands of said agents on account of said cruise." Riker's brother Abraham was captain of the marines aboard the *Yorktown*. Abraham drowned in the East River in 1813.

The *Saratoga*, one of the biggest privateers in the Port of New York, with sixteen guns and 140 men,[382] was reported to be "the best privateer fitted out of any port in the United States."[383] Between 1812 and 1815, the *Saratoga* captured twenty-two British ships.[384] Riker captained the ship on its first voyage. After capturing an enemy-flagged vessel, Riker would bring his captured ships to Rikers Island before heading into New York City and the prize court. This practice was highly lucrative—for example, the *Quebec*, which the *Saratoga* captured, carried cargo estimated to be worth $300,000 (roughly $6.2 million today).[385] Of course, the government took a large cut of the proceeds, but the privateer ship owner and crew shared the rest. Riker's second ship, the *Yorktown*, had twenty guns and 140 men.[386] The *Yorktown* captured six armed British ships before being captured by a British squadron off the coast of Newfoundland.[387] The *Yorktown* was brought to the Halifax prize court, where it suffered the same fate as those it had previously captured. Riker died in Port au Prince in 1817. He was forty-six years old.

FUN FACT Captain Thomas Masterman Hardy, the British commander of the *Ramillies* and its accompanying ships, had been the commanding officer on Lord Horatio Nelson's flagship *Victory* during the Battle of Trafalgar.

RICHARD RIKER
(SEPTEMBER 9, 1773–SEPTEMBER 26, 1842)

Andrew's younger brother Richard had a far more nefarious history. It started innocuously enough—he studied under Reverend John Witherspoon (at what later became Princeton) and qualified as a lawyer in 1795.[388] From 1802 through 1815, Richard Riker was elected to be New York City's first

Richard Riker Esq.
Recorder 1815-1819,1821-'23,1824-'38.

Richard Riker, originally published in the 1870 *Manual of the Corporation of the City of New York. Wikimedia Commons.*

district attorney and then city recorder (the municipal officer in charge of the criminal courts). He married Janet Phoenix in 1807, and together, they had six children. Recorder Riker and his wife moved in elite social circles, socializing with New York governor DeWitt Clinton and entertaining the likes of General Marquis de Lafayette during his 1824 visit to the United States.[389]

However, Richard Riker was involved in perpetuating slavery both personally and professionally. He personally enslaved at least one person—Jack Francis—until 1808 (similarly, DeWitt Clinton also enslaved at least one person named Massa until 1810, just before he was elected mayor of New York City).[390] Yet it was Riker's professional activities that cast the darkest shadow over New York City. During the decades before the Civil War, Recorder Riker became infamous for abusing the Fugitive Slave Act and selling free Black New Yorkers into slavery.[391] He did this as part of the Kidnapping Club,[392] a gang of complicit police officers and judges. As the City's recorder, Riker used his position to declare Black people "runaway slaves" without allowing them the opportunity to prove that they were actually free.[393] Since his signature as recorder was required on manumission certificates issued within the City, Riker clearly knew the falsity of many claims he upheld.

Abolitionist David Ruggles, head of the New York Vigilance Committee, frequently condemned Recorder Riker for his participation in schemes to enslave free Black New Yorkers for profit and for his role in sending those fleeing slavery back to the South.[394] Presaging the racially polarized role that Rikers Island would play in modern New York history, Riker was viewed as "the spider at the center of a web of injustice" by Black New Yorkers of his day,[395] while in the eyes of his white contemporaries Riker was a "good, kind-hearted judge,"[396] a near-saintly man[397] who was "the last man to wound by word or manner."[398]

The Riker family owned Rikers Island until 1884, when New York City's Commission of Charities and Corrections purchased the island for $180,000 for use as a jail. This purchase, which was authorized by then-governor Grover Cleveland,[399] was jurisdictionally complicated because the island was

NOT-SO-FUN FACT The island was originally 87.1 acres. However, at the time of purchase, the plan was to "reclaim" the shoals off the island and expand the island to 481.5 acres. Barge-loads of coal waste from Manhattan provided the fill, and the Department of Corrections forced inmates to do the hard labor necessary to expand the island to its current size.* Neighbors immediately began complaining about the unbearable odors, despite the City's suggestions that the odors, if they existed, were so beneficial to health that the island "should have a reputation as a health resort."†

---

* Jayne Mooney and Jarrod Shanahan, New York City's Captive Work Force: Remembering the Prisoners Who Built Rikers, 56 Int'l J. L., Crime & Just. 13 (2019).
† Defends Riker's Island Odors, N.Y. Times (Dec. 19, 1894); Rikers Island Use as Dump Denounced, N.Y. Times (Nov. 27, 1938); Rikers Island Dumping Nuisance, N.Y. Times (Jul. 8, 1894); Fumes a Problem at Jail: Board Finds Rikers Island Will Not Be Habitable If Dump Fires Continue, N.Y. Times (Oct. 29, 1931).

technically part of Long Island City, an entirely separate municipality. The purchase set off a jurisdictional dispute between Long Island City, Queens County and New York City that was only resolved in 1897, when Queens became part of New York City.

Since 1932, Rikers Island has housed New York City's main jail for men. One of the largest correctional facilities in the world, Rikers Island gained notoriety for abuse and neglect of prisoners. In May 2013, Rikers Island was ranked as one of the ten worst prisons in the United States. The next year, U.S. attorney Preet Bharara issued a scathing report on the "deep-seated culture of violence" among the guards and staff of the Rikers Island Correctional Center and identified systemic institutional deficiencies responsible for pervasive violence.[400] In April 2017, New York City mayor DeBlasio announced plans to close the prison at Rikers Island, and in the fall of 2019, New York City Council voted to close Rikers Island. In the spring of 2021, New York City Council enacted a trio of bills known as Renewable Rikers that will turn the island into a hub for renewable energy and urban sustainability.

Chapter 3

PETER COOPER

THE INVETERATE TINKERER

Cooper Union is named after its founder, industrialist and inventor Peter Cooper (1791–1883). Manhattan's Peter Cooper Village is also named in his honor.

FAMILY LIFE

Peter Cooper. *Wikimedia Commons.*

Peter Cooper's life is truly a rags-to-riches story. Born in New York City to Margaret Campbell and John Cooper, Peter Cooper attended only one year of school and never received a formal education. As a child, Cooper worked with his hatmaker father and later was apprenticed to a coach-maker. An inveterate tinkerer, Cooper also worked as a cabinetmaker, a brewer, a grocer and a glue-maker. His inventions span the gamut between blast furnace, washing machine, torpedo boat and musical cradle.

Cooper's first successful business venture was selling the cloth-shearing machine he designed and patented. During the War of 1812, when trade with Britain was disrupted, this machine was in high demand.

In 1813, Cooper married Sarah Bedell. Together, they had six children, only two of whom lived to adulthood.

COMMERCIAL SUCCESS

---

* Jasmine K. Williams, Peter Cooper: A Champion for Education, N.Y. Post (Jan. 5, 2007).

After the war ended, Cooper worked as a grocer. He was again successful and used his profits to purchase a glue-making factory in Kips Bay, New York. Cooper invested the profits from his enterprises by purchasing a large tract of land in Baltimore, Maryland, and made his first fortune selling iron from deposits found on this land. With two partners, he established the Canton Iron Works, which made rails for the Baltimore and Ohio Railroad. Looking to drum up business and demonstrate the potential of steam-powered rail transit in America, Cooper built the prototype Tom Thumb locomotive—the first locomotive constructed in the United States. To combat skepticism about whether trains could navigate curves, Cooper ran a series of "proof of concept" rides, including a race

Replica of the Tom Thumb locomotive. *Library of Congress.*

against a horse-drawn carriage.[401] Although a boiler leak caused Cooper's train to lose the race, his point was made, and railroads quickly became an indispensable form of transportation.

In 1855, Cooper helped found the American Telegraphic Company. Under his tenure as president, the company dominated America's rapidly expanding telegraph network. Just three years later, Cooper helped supervise the laying of the first transatlantic telegraph cable.[402] Having made fortunes in real estate, iron and steel, railroads and telecommunications, Cooper became one of the wealthiest men in America.

FUN FACT Cooper held the very first American patent for the manufacture of a portable gelatin dessert that required only the addition of hot water (U.S. Patent 4084). In 1895, Cooper sold the patent to a cough syrup manufacturer, who added flavored sugar to Cooper's prepackaged gelatin and began marketing the resulting powder under the name Jell-O.*

---

* History of Gelatin, Gelatine, and Jell-O, whatscookingamerica.net/History/Jell-0-history.htm.

COOPER UNION

Despite his vast wealth, Cooper lived modestly and devoted himself to social and philanthropic causes. He was deeply influenced by his Unitarian Universalist faith. In 1859, he founded the Cooper Union for the Advancement of Science and Art with a mission to provide education that was free and open to all talented young people. Cooper believed that education should be "free as water and air." To that end, the school charged no tuition until 2014, and from its inception, Cooper Union had an admissions policy that prohibited discrimination on the basis of race, religion or gender.

FUN FACT In 1860, Peter Cooper served with James Lenox (*see entry on Lenox*) and other New York luminaries on a committee tasked with making arrangements for a dinner showcasing "grace and beauty, as well as the wealth and enterprise of New York," for the visiting Prince of Wales.*

---

* The Prince of Wales in New-York, N.Y. Times (Aug. 15, 1860).

In one of its first events, Abraham Lincoln spoke at Cooper Institute in 1860, giving what came to be known as his "Right Makes Might" speech. William Cullen Bryant (*see entry on Bryant*) introduced Lincoln. The speech, which laid out the Republican case against expansion of slavery into the territories, sparked an electric reaction from the cheering audience. The closing line of the speech exhorted the crowd, "Let us have faith that right makes might, and in that faith, let us, to the end, dare to do our duty as we understand it."

Publisher Horace Greeley immediately published the full text of the speech on the front page of the *New York Tribune*.[403] The *New York Times* also published the entire speech.[404] A pamphlet of Lincoln's speech went through five printings and was widely circulated by his campaign.

POLITICS

Peter Cooper was active in the antislavery movement before the Civil War and was a strong supporter of the Union cause. After his death, the Cooper Institute helped organize the National Association for the Advancement of Colored People (NAACP).

Cooper also took a strong stand on "the Indian Question." Working with abolitionist Henry Ward Beecher, Cooper formed and funded the United States Indian Commission, a private organization dedicated to "the protection and elevation" of Native Americans and the elimination of warfare in the western territories. The commission drafted an 1868 memorial to Congress declaring "that our aboriginal inhabitants have been the victims of great wrongs, cruelties, and outrage" and calling for "the most prompt and vigorous measures of redress and remedy."[405] Cooper personally sponsored delegations from the western tribes to Washington, D.C., and the Cooper Institute ensured that Arapaho, Cheyenne, Sioux and

Greenback Bank of Bread. *Courtesy of Heritage Auction and Cooper Union Archives.*

Wichita leaders had a forum to speak about the violence and deprivation they faced.[406] Cooper was a strong advocate of citizenship for Indians. However, the commission's advocacy ultimately morphed into the discredited United States' Indian boarding school policy, which involved the forced removal and education of Indian children.

A passionate opponent of the gold standard, Cooper ran for president as the Greenback Party candidate in 1876. Cooper was eighty-five—making him the oldest person ever nominated for president by a political party in the United States. He came in a distant third behind Rutherford B. Hayes and Samuel Tilden. The Hayes-Tilden compromise, which settled the disputed election, ended Reconstruction in the South and led directly to Jim Crow segregation policies.

Cooper died in 1883 at the age of ninety-two. By a resolution of city council, his body lay in state in the Governor's Room at city hall. Twelve thousand mourners viewed his body, while thousands more lined the streets. Flags flew at half-mast in his honor, and bells rang as his body was escorted to Greenwood Cemetery in Brooklyn.

FUN FACT Peter Cooper lived through twenty-one presidential administrations. When he was born, George Washington was president, and he died during Chester Arthur's presidency.

Chapter 4

HERBERT LEHMAN

FDR'S GOOD RIGHT HAND

L ehman College was named after Herbert Henry Lehman (March 28, 1878–December 5, 1963), who served as governor and senator from New York.

FAMILY LIFE

Herbert Lehman was born in New York City in 1878 to Jewish parents Mayer Lehman and Babette Newgass Lehmen. His father, Mayer, emigrated from Bavaria with his brothers Henry and Emanuel. The three brothers settled first in the South, where they became deeply entangled in the slave-era cotton trade. Mayer supported the South during the Civil War and, according to the 1860 census, personally enslaved seven people. Rather than enlist in the Confederate army, Mayer worked as a blockade runner maneuvering cotton through Northern blockades. After the war, Mayer moved to New York, where he organized the New York Cotton Exchange and co-founded Lehman Brothers, the investment bank whose 2008 collapse triggered a global economic crisis. In 1858, Mayer married Babette in New Orleans. Together, Babette and Mayer had eight children; Herbert was their youngest.

Lehman grew up in a very wealthy family. He lived with his parents and siblings in a five-story brownstone near Central Park. Lehman attended the prestigious Sachs Collegiate Institute (now the Dwight School) before

Herbert H. Lehman. *Library of Congress.*

enrolling in Williams College. He graduated from Williams in 1899 and began working in the textile industry. A decade later, Lehman joined the family firm as a partner in Lehman Brothers in 1909. Soon after, he married Edith Louise Altschul, whose father was the managing partner of the Lazard Freres & Company investment bank. Together, they had three children. Their eldest, Peter, died in action in World War II.

During World War I, Lehman was too old for the draft. He instead served in a civilian capacity as aide to Assistant Secretary of the Navy Franklin D. Roosevelt before being commissioned a captain in the United States Army.[407] Lehman was rapidly promoted to the rank of colonel, ultimately serving as an aide to General George Goethals on the War Department General Staff (*see entry on Goethals*). In 1919, Lehman was awarded the U.S. Distinguished Service Medal for this work. Prompted by his experiences touring devastated parts of Europe after the war, Lehman helped found the American Jewish Joint Distribution Committee. Lehman remained

FUN FACT Babette dominated her family, involving herself in every aspect of her children's lives and her husband's business. She was reportedly his most trusted adviser. At her death in 1920, Babette left a personal estate of $2 million ($23.7 million in today's dollars).

active in philanthropic and social justice causes throughout his career, serving, inter alia, on the board of Lillian Wald's Henry Street Settlement House and the NAACP. For his war service and his philanthropic endeavors, Lehman's alma mater, Williams, awarded him an honorary doctorate in 1929.[408] Edith later also received an honorary doctorate from Williams in recognition of her lifelong philanthropic work.

POLITICS

Lehman and Roosevelt reunited in 1928 as running mates for governor and lieutenant governor of New York. Lehman and Roosevelt worked closely together, with Governor Roosevelt referring to Lehman as "that good right arm of mine."[409] When FDR became the 1932 Democratic presidential candidate, Lehman ran for governor. He was elected in a landslide victory. He served four terms as New York State's forty-fifth governor, winning elections in 1932, 1934 (defeating Robert Moses), 1936 and 1938. Lehman is the only governor to have been elected to four successive terms.

FUN FACT During the 1936 Democratic National Convention, Lehman gave the main speech seconding Roosevelt's nomination for president.

As governor, Lehman pushed a "Little New Deal" through a somewhat hostile legislature. Under this program, Lehman supported unemployment insurance, minimum wages and workers' compensation, among other progressive causes.

From 1943 until 1946, Lehman was the inaugural director of the United Nations Relief and Rehabilitation Administration. In that capacity, he directed the largest international relief effort in history: twenty-four million tons of food, clothing and medical supplies to 500 million victims of world war. He was honored across the globe for this work, receiving, among other accolades, the Order of the Auspicious Star Grand Cordon from the Chinese government.[410]

Lehman was elected to the United States Senate in a 1949 special election after Senator Robert Wagner resigned due to ill health.[411] It was a hard-fought race, and Lehman's opponent John Foster Dulles resorted to racist and antisemitic dog whistles in his quest to defeat Lehman.[412] Lehman won. Lehman was then elected to a full term in 1950. Known as "the conscience of the Senate," Lehman was an early and outspoken opponent of McCarthyism. He was the only senator seeking reelection to vote against

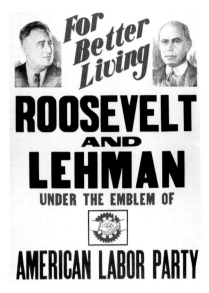

For Better Living

ROOSEVELT AND LEHMAN

UNDER THE EMBLEM OF

AMERICAN LABOR PARTY

Lehman and Roosevelt, American Labor Party. *Wikimedia Commons.*

the McCarran Internal Security Act, declaring, "I will not compromise with my conscience....I shall cast my vote to protect the liberties of our people."[413] Lehman won reelection anyway. As senator, Lehman fought against restrictive immigrant quotas, for worker protection and for the protection of voting rights. In 1957, at age seventy-eight, Lehman declined to run for a third term and retired from the Senate. He did not, however, retire from public life. After his retirement from the Senate, Lehman worked with Eleanor Roosevelt to reform the New York Democratic Party and end the grip of Tammany Hall.

In 1963, President John F. Kennedy nominated Herbert Lehman to be among the initial honorees receiving the new Presidential Medal of Freedom for distinguished civilian service in peace time. The medals were originally intended to be presented in September 1963. However, delays in striking the medals meant the event was postponed until early December. President Kennedy was assassinated

FUN FACT In 1960, Herbert and Edith celebrated their fiftieth wedding anniversary by donating $500,000 to establish a children's zoo in Central Park. The plan was to allow children to pet and feed "tame," "peaceful animals," including perhaps a talking crow.[*] The Lehman Zoo had a sign declaring, "No Adult Will Be Admitted unless Accompanied by a Child." Today, only the fanciful gate remains from the original Lehman Zoo. In 1997, Henry and Edith Everett withdrew a planned $3 million donation to refurbish and rename Lehman Zoo when the New York City Arts Commission ruled that plaques acknowledging the Lehmans' original gift would remain on the gate, relegating the plaque acknowledging the Everetts to a less desirable spot. The Tisch family stepped in to replace the withdrawn gift, and the zoo is now known as the Tisch Zoo.[†]

---

[*] Lehmans Give City Zoo for Children, N.Y. Times (Jun. 6, 1960).
[†] Judith Miller, Tisch to Match, Raise Revoked Gift to Children's Zoo, N.Y. Times (May 20, 1997).

on November 22, 1963. President Lyndon B. Johnson decided that the occasion should go forward as scheduled on December 6, 1963. Tragically, on the morning of December 5, as Herbert Lehman prepared to leave for the ceremony in Washington, he suffered a heart attack and died.[414] The president and Ladybird Johnson attended his funeral at Emanu-El synagogue, where Lehman's father, Mayer, had been a longtime board member. The medal was presented posthumously to his wife, Edith.[415]

After his death, Edith started the Mount Sinai Hospital Medical School in his honor. In 1968, the Bronx campus of Hunter College, now part of CUNY, was renamed Lehman College in his honor. Lehman College is consistently ranked as one of the top schools promoting social mobility in the United States.[416]

FUN FACT The campus of Lehman College served as the first home of the United Nations, with the gym serving as chambers for the UN Security Council and the Social and Economic Council.*

* Crystal Nix, U.N. in Bronx: Recalling Exciting Early Days, N.Y. Times (Oct. 20, 1985).

Chapter 5

ARCHIBALD GRACIE

THE SHIPPING MAGNATE

Gracie Mansion, the mayor of New York City's official residence, was built in 1799 by Scottish-born merchant Archibald Gracie (1755–1829).

FAMILY LIFE

Archibald Gracie was born in Dumfries, Scotland, on June 25, 1755, to parents William and Mary Gracie. His father, William, was a weaver. In 1776, Gracie left Scotland for Liverpool, where he found work with a Dutch West India Company firm. The ambitious Gracie worked himself up to the position of chief clerk. Having saved some capital, Gracie invested in a share of a ship and its cargo. With his investment, he sailed for New York.

Gracie arrived in 1784, shortly after the American Revolution. That same year, he married Esther (Hetitia) Rogers.[417] Together, they had ten children. Within a few years,

Archibald Gracie. *Courtesy of the Gracie Mansion Conservancy.*

Gracie had moved his growing family to Petersburg, Virginia. The Gracies spent eight years in Virginia, where Gracie shipped tobacco and built a fortune by participating in the slavery economy.

When Gracie returned to New York City for good in 1793, he brought back with him an enslaved couple, Sarah and Abram Short. A decade later, Gracie signed emancipation papers for the couple and their son. Gracie then became active in the Manumission Society, which advocated to end slavery and educate Black New Yorkers.

MERCANTILE SUCCESS

At the same time, however, his successful mercantile company, Archibald Gracie and Sons, continued to trade goods related to the slavery economy. Gracie's commercial ventures included shipping partnerships with Robert Lenox (*see entry on Lenox*). For many years, Gracie's fleet of twenty-one cargo ships was the largest in New York.[418] Indeed, Gracie was commonly considered one of New York's "merchant princes."[419]

Gracie rapidly became both powerful and influential in New York's economic circles. He helped found the Eagle Insurance Company; was vice president of the New York Insurance Company; was an original shareholder in the Tontine Association, the precursor to the New York Stock Exchange; and spent two decades as vice president of the New York Chamber of Commerce, which he also helped to found. From 1818 to 1823, Gracie was president of the St. Andrews Society. Notably, Gracie was also a director for the Bank of the United States, the banking institution that figured prominently in Macomb's financial schemes (*see entry on Macomb*). Gracie's eldest grandchild, Caroline Gracie Duer, was married to the son of Macomb's collaborator in that scheme, William Duer.

Although the Gracies maintained a principal residence down at the tip of Manhattan, in 1799, they built a two-story summer home roughly five miles north (at what is now 88th Street and East End Avenue, overlooking the East River at Hells Gate). Gracie Mansion was almost certainly built, at least in part, by the labor of enslaved people. The neighborhood was a swanky one—Gracie's neighbors included John Jacob Astor (*see entry on Astor*) and the infamous recorder Richard Riker (*see entry on Riker*). Their house had a spectacular view of Hells Gate, a particularly treacherous portion of the East River.

In 1811, the Gracies significantly expanded and renovated Gracie Mansion. Architect Major Charles Pierre L'Enfant, who planned Washington, D.C., helped design at least part of the renovation. The enlarged, elegantly furnished mansion provided an ideal backdrop for the many parties Gracie and his wife hosted. For a brief time, the Gracies routinely welcomed such illustrious guests as Alexander Hamilton, John Quincy Adams, John Jay, Washington Irving and Louis Philippe, the exiled king of France. At the behest of Alexander Hamilton, Gracie once hosted a Federalist meeting at his mansion to raise $10,000 for the founding of the *New York Evening Post* (now the *New York Post*). To this day, the paper counts Gracie and Hamilton among its founders.

FUN FACT The year after Hamilton's fateful duel with Aaron Burr, Gracie joined with Astor (*see entry on Astor*), Robert Lenox (*see entry on Lenox*) and other Federalists to create an $80,000 secret fund to support Hamilton's family and keep them in their home, the Grange.*

* Josephine Mayer and Robert A. East, The Settlement of Alexander Hamilton's Debts: A Footnote to History, 18 N.Y. Hist. 378 (1937).

FINANCIAL COLLAPSE

Unfortunately for Gracie, Jefferson's Embargo Act of 1807, which prohibited American ships from engaging in virtually all foreign trade, hit his business hard. Even though the act was repealed in 1809, the damage to Gracie's mercantile interests was lasting. During that same period, Napoleon's forces captured two of Gracie's vessels laden with gold and other valuables.[420] Gracie sought to have Congress exert pressure to get the French to pay him compensation for these lost ships. However, it took until the Jackson administration for the claims to be settled, and by then, Gracie was long dead.

The War of 1812 further hurt Gracie's trading interests, with the British capturing many of his ships. The bank instability during the Panic of 1819 damaged what was left of Gracie's wealth. In 1817, much of Gracie's property was auctioned to satisfy the mortgages on his real estate. Gracie's friend and business partner Robert Lenox purchased a large parcel of Gracie's land at auction for $6,420—far more than the parcel was worth at the time.[421] (For perspective, Lenox bought an adjacent parcel from the City for $500.) These acres became known as Lenox Farm (*see entry on Lenox*).

Gracie's dire financial situation forced him to part with Gracie Mansion. New York senator Rufus King, whose sons James Gore King and Charles King were married to Gracie's daughters Sarah and Eliza, took legal possession of the mansion in 1819, probably as compensation for unpaid loans King had made in an attempt to save Gracie's business. Nevertheless, Gracie continued to live at the mansion until 1823, when King sold Gracie Mansion to shipping magnate Joseph Foulke.

Archibald Gracie died on April 11, 1829. He was seventy-four.

GRACIE MANSION

As leaseholder of the island of Bonaire, Foulke made his fortune by deforesting the entire island and by exploiting the labor of 300 enslaved people. Foulke lived in Gracie Mansion until his death in 1852. In 1857, the property was sold to Noah Wheaton. In 1896, the City of New York seized Gracie Mansion from Wheaton's estate for nonpayment of taxes.

For decades, Gracie Mansion was used as a concession stand and restroom for Carl Schurz Park along the East River. The house fell into disrepair. In 1922, the New York legislature vested the Patriotic New Yorkers Society—an organization founded and led by one of Gracie's great-grandchildren, May Denning King van Rensselaer—with the task of preserving and maintaining the mansion.[422] Under their auspices, Gracie Mansion became the first home for the Museum of the City of New York in 1923.

When the museum moved to its current location on 5th Avenue, Parks Commissioner Robert Moses restored the mansion and proposed it as the official residence for New York City's mayor. He met with fierce opposition from then-mayor Fiorello LaGuardia (*see entry on LaGuardia*), who was reluctant to leave his personal residence in an East Harlem tenement. However, after

Gracie Mansion. *Photo by Jim Henderson, Wikimedia Commons.*

Pearl Harbor, Moses persuaded LaGuardia to move on the theory that Gracie Mansion's riverside location would make evacuation easier should the Nazis bomb New York City. LaGuardia moved into Gracie Mansion in 1942.

Nearly every mayor since LaGuardia has lived in Gracie Mansion. The only exceptions have been billionaire Michael Bloomberg, who remained in his nearby personal townhouse, and Rudy Giuliani, who moved out after a judge barred him from bringing his girlfriend, Judith Nathan, to the mansion during his messy divorce proceeding.[423] Part of Gracie Mansion is a museum open to the public. In 1964, Mayor Wagner added an entire wing to the house in order to better preserve the distinction between private residence and public functions. The wing, known as the Susan Wagner Wing, was named for his wife, who died during its construction. In 1975, Gracie Mansion was added to the National Register of Historic Places.[424]

FUN FACT Gracie's great-grandson Colonel Archibald Gracie IV was the last survivor to leave the sinking *Titanic*. Colonel Gracie helped rescue dozens of his fellow passengers. Gracie was haunted by the disaster and never fully recovered from the ordeal. He died a year later, and his dying words were, "We must get them into the boats. We must get them all into the boats."*

---

* Col. Gracie Dies Haunted by Titanic, N.Y. Times (Dec. 5, 1919).

Chapter 6

FIORELLO LAGUARDIA

HIZZONER THE MAYOR

LaGuardia Airport was named after New York City's ninety-ninth mayor, Fiorello LaGuardia (December 11, 1882–September 20, 1947). LaGuardia served three terms as mayor of New York City, from 1934 to 1945, and is widely acclaimed as one of the greatest mayors in American history.[425] In his obituary, the *New York Times* called him "New York's most colorful Mayor since Peter Stuyvesant."[426] He was also one of the shortest. Only five feet tall, LaGuardia was called "the fiery little man with the black hat,"[427] as well as "Hizzoner" and "Little Flower" (the literal translation of *Fiorello*).

FAMILY LIFE

LaGuardia was born on December 11, 1882, in New York City's Greenwich Village. Both his parents were immigrants; his father, Achille LaGuardia, came from Cerignola, Italy, and his mother, Irene Luzzatto Coen, came from Trieste, then part of the Austro-Hungarian empire. Although his mother was Jewish and his father was Catholic, LaGuardia was raised Episcopalian.

In addition to English, LaGuardia spoke German, French, Italian, Croatian, Hungarian and Yiddish. Drawing on these language skills, LaGuardia joined the State Department at a young age and worked in multiple European consulates. He returned to New York in 1907 to attend NYU Law School, attending at night and working as a Bureau of

Young Fiorello LaGuardia.
Wikimedia Commons.

Immigration interpreter at Ellis Island during the day. After graduating from law school in 1910, LaGuardia was admitted to the bar and began representing immigrant garment workers in court.

On March 8, 1919, LaGuardia married Thea Almerigotti. Together, they had one daughter, Fioretta. Tragically, both Thea and Fioretta died of tubercular meningitis in 1921. In 1929, LaGuardia married for a second time, wedding his longtime secretary, Marie Fisher. Together, the couple adopted two children—a boy named Eric and a girl named Jean—who were the first children to live in Gracie Mansion in its incarnation as the mayor's residence (*see entry on Gracie*).

POLITICS

LaGuardia was elected to Congress in 1916, representing Manhattan's Fourteenth Congressional District. He was the first Republican to hold this Tammany Hall–dominated seat since the Civil War. When the United States entered World War I, LaGuardia promised the young men in his district that if he voted to draft them, he would also serve.[428] True to his word, in 1917, LaGuardia obtained a leave of absence from Congress and served as a first lieutenant in the U.S. Army Air Service. He was stationed in Italy. During the war, he was promoted to captain and then to major. He wound up commanding the United States Air Forces on the Italian-Austrian front and served as the army representative on the Joint Army and Navy Aircraft Committee in Italy. For his service, LaGuardia was awarded the Italian War Cross.

LaGuardia was reelected to Congress in 1918 while still in uniform. After the Armistice, LaGuardia resigned his military commission. He returned to take up his seat in the final session of the Sixty-First Congress. The next year, LaGuardia ran for the New York City Board of Alderman seat that became vacant when Al Smith was elected governor. LaGuardia won, becoming the first Republican to win a citywide office since the 1896 creation of a unified New York City. He resigned his congressional seat and served as president of the New York City Board of Aldermen in 1920 and 1921.

LaGuardia was reelected to Congress in 1923, this time representing East Harlem's Twentieth Congressional District. He won on the Socialist ticket and was then reelected four times as a Republican. All his life, LaGuardia championed progressive causes like labor rights and women's suffrage. He vocally opposed child labor and prohibition. He was associated with some of the most progressive legislation in Congress, including the Labor Anti-Injunction Act. He was a vocal opponent of Nazism and antisemitism.

THE MAYOR

In 1929, LaGuardia lost the election for mayor of New York City to incumbent Democrat Jimmy Walker by a landslide. When Walker was forced to resign on corruption charges in 1932, LaGuardia ran for mayor again, this time winning a hard-fought three-way race.

For the next decade, LaGuardia dominated city politics. He was an outspoken opponent of organized crime, which profited heavily from Prohibition, and gambling. Indeed, his first action as mayor was to order the chief of police to arrest mob boss Lucky Luciano on whatever charges could be found. As part of an anti–organized crime campaign during his first

FUN FACT In 1942, LaGuardia waged a similar war on pinball machines. Calling their owners "slimy crews of tinhorns, well dressed and living in luxury on penny thievery," LaGuardia ordered the city police to make pinball raids their top priority. Hizzoner personally smashed seized pinball machines with a sledgehammer.

year in office, LaGuardia led a crackdown on slot machines, which were an illegal but widely tolerated form of gambling. LaGuardia went so far as to personally smash the first slot machines, which he then ritually tossed into Long Island Sound.

When LaGuardia took office in 1934, New York was mired in the Great Depression. LaGuardia forged a close working relationship with President Roosevelt. He maintained a direct line of communication with the president's "Brain Trust," and New York City often served as a laboratory for New Deal policies.[429] New Deal funding helped build the Triborough Bridge, LaGuardia Airport, FDR Drive and the Lincoln Tunnel, as well as schools, parks and murals across the city. By the time LaGuardia retired in 1945, he left the city revitalized and optimistic. In the process, LaGuardia made his mark on virtually every aspect of New York City, unifying the transit system, reorganizing the sanitation and police departments, building low-cost public housing and constructing airports. Above all, LaGuardia restored public faith in City government by ending patronage hiring and routing the Tammany Hall machine.

In 1940, Yale University granted LaGuardia an honorary doctorate of law, stating that LaGuardia had "taken democracy from the politicians and given it back to the people."[430] LaGuardia was in good company—the poet Carl Sandburg, the theologian Paul Tillich and the Chinese ambassador Hu Shih received honorary Yale degrees at the same time.

New York Municipal Airport, Marine Air Terminal. *Library of Congress.*

FUN FACT Soon after he was elected mayor, LaGuardia refused to get off a Washington–New York flight that landed at New Jersey's Newark Airport. LaGuardia insisted that he had purchased a ticket to a New York airport. He was finally flown to Floyd Bennett Field in Brooklyn. Largely a publicity gimmick, LaGuardia's grandstanding resulted in New York City building a municipal airport in Queens to compete with Newark. The airport was named LaGuardia Airport in 1953.

Left: Fiorello LaGuardia. *Photo by Fred Palumbo,* World Telegram *staff photographer, Wikimedia Commons.*

Right: LaGuardia stamp, USPS. *Wikimedia Commons.*

As mayor, La Guardia had a regular Sunday radio show on WNYC called *Talk to the People*. During the 1945 newspaper delivery strike, LaGuardia famously encouraged parents to gather their children around the radio. Hizzoner then proceeded to read *Dick Tracy* and other comics to his radio audience.

In 1942, LaGuardia designated Gracie Mansion (*see entry on Gracie*) as the official residence of the New York City mayor.

After leaving the mayor's office in 1945, LaGuardia was appointed director general for the United Nations Relief and Rehabilitation Administration in 1946, succeeding Herbert Lehman (*see entry on Lehman*). In that capacity, LaGuardia oversaw distribution of billions of dollars in aid to war victims and refugees. One of the people he aided was his own sister Gemma La Guardia Gluck, who had been living in Italy and was imprisoned by the Nazis in the Ravensbrück concentration camp.[431] LaGuardia's brother-in-law Herman Gluck was murdered by Nazis in the Mauthausen concentration camp.

LaGuardia died of pancreatic cancer in 1947. He was sixty-four. Before his funeral, his body lay in state at the Cathedral of St. John the Divine. More than 45,000 New Yorkers waited in line for hours to pay their respects and pass by his open coffin.[432] After the funeral, more than 130 police officers and 20 motorcycle police escorted the funeral cortege to Woodlawn

FUN FACT LaGuardia was the first Italian American to be elected to the U.S. Congress and the second to be elected mayor of a major United States city (Mayor Rossi of San Francisco was the first). As mayor, LaGuardia gave America another first: his 1939 appointment of Yale Law School graduate Jane Bolin to the New York City Domestic Relations Court gave the United States its first Black woman judge.

Cemetery in the Bronx, following a route that passed over Macomb's Dam Bridge (*see entry on Macomb*).

In addition to LaGuardia Airport, LaGuardia Community College, LaGuardia School of Performing Arts and LaGuardia Square in Greenwich Village are all named after him. He was also memorialized on a fourteen-cent United States postage stamp.

NOTES

Introduction

1. Robert Moses, *Natural and Proper Home of the U.N.*, N.Y. TIMES (Oct. 20, 1946).
2. ROBERT CARO, THE POWER BROKER 909–910 (1974).
3. Robert Moses, *Its Going to Be Quite a Town*, N.Y. TIMES (Feb. 16, 1947).

Part I

4. *Suit for Double Divorce*, N.Y. TIMES (Jul. 18, 1919).
5. *Man and Affinity Desert Old Mates*, THE SUN (Jul. 18, 1919).
6. *Delegates to State Convention Show Resentment Toward Outside Influences by Electing Deegan 423–77*, N.Y. TRIB. (Oct. 9, 1921).
7. *Obtain 3 Hospitals for Servicemen*, N.Y. TIMES (Jun. 19, 1922).
8. *Veterans Plight Laid to Politicians*, N.Y. TIMES (Mar. 29, 1922); *Legion Commander Suggests Reliable Veterans to Guard Payroll*, N.Y. TIMES (March 17, 1922); *Legion Commander Wants Employers to Place Ex-Servicemen*, N.Y. TIMES (Dec. 7, 1921).
9. *Col. Forbes Orders Inquiry on Hospital*, N.Y. HERALD (Sept. 8, 1922).
10. *Legionaires in All Parts of the U.S Will Indorse William F. Deegan for the Office of National Commander*, N.Y. TRIB. (Oct. 12, 1922).
11. *Veterans Bureau Head, at New Orleans Convention, Answers Charges by Deegan*, N.Y. TIMES (Oct. 15, 1922).
12. *Major Deegan Explains*, N.Y. TIMES (Feb. 10, 1928).
13. W.W. Foster, *A Letter and a Reply in Which We Attempt to Explain the "Other Side" of the 7-cent Fare Controversy*, PITTSBURGH PRESS (Feb. 15, 1928).

14. For a contemporary account of the reasons behind the tenement code, *see* Robert W. de Forest, *Tenement House Regulation: The Reasons for It: Its Proper Limitations*, 20 Annals Am. Acad. Pol. and Soc. Sci. 83–95 (1902).

15. *Deegan Reports on Law Violations*, N.Y. Times (Apr. 17, 1931).

16. *Doyle Must Testify or Face Jail Today*, N.Y. Times (Jul. 21, 1931).

17. *Walker's Statement Explaining His Decision to Resign as Mayor*, N.Y. Times (Sept. 2, 1932).

18. *Walker's Love of Betty Compton Weathered Many Political and Social Storms*, Times-Union Albany (Apr. 19, 1933).

19. *Deegan Collapses from Overwork*, N.Y. Times (Jul. 17, 1930).

20. *Military Funeral for Major Deegan*, N.Y. Times (Apr. 5, 1932).

21. *Highway Proposed for Van Courtland*, N.Y. Times (Jun. 12, 1947).

22. Andrew Sinclair, The Emancipation of the American Woman 23 (1966).

23. Lyle Koehler, *The Case of the American Jezebels: Anne Hutchinson and Female Agitation During the Years of Antinomian Turmoil*, 31 Wm. and Mary Q. 55, 57 (Jan. 1974).

24. Charles Francis Adams, Antinomianism in the Colony of Massachusetts Bay 1636–1638 (1894).

25. John Winthrop, *A Short Story of the Rise, Reign, and Ruine of the Antinomians, Familists and Libertines*, reproduced in Antinomianism in the Colony of Massachusetts Bay 232.

26. *Id.*

27. Eve LaPlante, American Jezebel (2005).

28. Koehler, *supra* note 24 at 64–66.

29. David D. Hall, The Antinomian Controversy 1636–1638 xi (1999).

30. Carol F. Karlsen, The Devil in the Shape of a Woman (1998).

31. Transcript of the Trial of Anne Hutchinson, www.swarthmore.edu/SocSci/bdorsey1/41docs/30-hut.html.

32. Deborah Crawford, Four Women in a Violent Time 137 (1970).

33. Michael J. Colacurcio, *Footsteps of Anne Hutchinson: The Context of the Scarlet Letter*, 39 ELH 459 (1972).

34. Dominico Annese, *The Impact of Parkway Development in Westchester County, New York City, and the Metropolitan New York Region*, in Greenways, Riverways, Parkways: Past and Future (1987).

35. Robert Caro, The Power Broker 318 (1974).

36. John Vernon, *Jim Crow, Meet Lieutenant Robinson*, Prologue, Vol 40 (Spring 2008).

37. Jackie Robinson, *Glad of Opportunity and Try to Make Good*, Pittsburgh Courier (Nov. 3, 1945).

38. Act to award a congressional gold medal to Jackie Robinson (posthumously), 117 Stat. 1195 §1(8) (2003).

39. *Jackie Robinson*, Baseball Reference, www.baseball-reference.com/players/r/robinja02.shtml.

40. 117 Stat. 1195, *supra* note 39.

41. Department of Transportation, State DOT Commissioner Announces Start of Paving on the Jackie Robinson Parkway (May 29, 2015).

42. TAMMANY TIMES (Nov. 5, 1900).

43. Rep. Henry Bruckner, www.govtrack.us/congress/members/henry_bruckner/401926.

44. Statement of Hon. Henry Bruckner, Hearing Before the Committee on Ways and Means on the Proposed Revenue Act of 1918, Part II, Miscellaneous Taxes, 1120–1125 (1918).

45. Official Gazette of the United States Patent Office, Vol. 290, p. 407.

46. *Seabury May Drop Plans to Jail Hastings*, BROOKLYN DAILY EAGLE (Apr. 10, 1932); *Cash Put Too Low, Bruckner Testifies*, N.Y. TIMES (Apr. 9, 1932); *Big Deposits Traced to Bronx President*, N.Y. TIMES (Apr. 5, 1932).

47. *Betty Compton Feels Sting of Seabury's Whip*, TUSCALOOSA NEWS (Dec. 20, 1932).

48. Jesse McKinley, *F.Y.I.*, N.Y. TIMES (Nov. 19, 1995) (quoting Bronx historian Lloyd Ultan).

49. *Seabury Report Scores Walker Administration*, LEWISTON DAILY SUN (Dec. 20, 1932).

50. *Flynn Inquiry Bares 5,000% Rakeoff*, BROOKLYN DAILY EAGLE (Mar. 15, 1932).

51. *Investigator Recommended Removal of Bruckner, Flynn and McKay*, LEWISTON DAILY SUN (Dec. 21, 1932).

52. *1000 Attend Mass for Henry Bruckner*, N.Y. TIMES (Apr. 18, 1942).

53. Municipal Civil Service of the City of New York, Minutes of the Commission 253 (1907).

54. *20,000 Troops Land at Newport News*, BROOKLYN DAILY EAGLE (May 1, 1919).

55. *Resolution Establishing Two Grades of Position of Assistant Engineer Under the President of the Borough of the Bronx*, Proceedings of the Board of Aldermen of the City of New York and Approved by the Mayor 803 (Nov. 23, 1920).

56. *City Engineers Press Campaign for Higher Pay*, DAILY STAR (Queens) (May 26, 1927).

57. *30,000 Lose Homes for Bronx Bri*dge, N.Y. TIMES (Jul. 22, 1937).

58. *Sheridan Succeeds Moran in the Bronx*, N.Y. TIMES (Jun. 9, 1942).

59. *Our Highways Seen Inadequate in War*, N.Y. TIMES (May 9, 1941).

60. *Underground City of Future Mapped*, N.Y. TIMES (Aug. 16, 1938).

61. CARO, supra note 2 at 861–865.

62. NSPE, *75 Years of Excellence* (2009) www.nspe.org/sites/default/files/resources/pdfs/NSPE75thAnniversary.pdf.

63. Peter Stuyvesant, *Fame Rushes by Engineers*, BROOKLYN DAILY EAGLE (1929).

64. *Engineers Warned of Labor Movement*, N.Y. TIMES (Oct. 9, 1937).

65. *Engineers Demand Place in Cabinet*, N.Y. TIMES (Mar. 17, 1935).

66. *A.V. Sheridan Gets Scroll*, N.Y. TIMES (May 5, 1946).

67. *A.V. Sheridan Dies in Auto Accident*, N.Y. TIMES (Jun. 20, 1952).

68. Manhattan College, Financial Assistance, catalog.manhattan.edu/undergraduate/financialservices/financialassistance.

69. *Engineer Dies in Auto Crash*, Ossining Citizen Reg. (Jun. 20, 1952).

70. *Call It Sheridan Expressway*, N.Y. Post (Feb. 18, 1953).

71. David W. Dunlap, *Why Robert Moses Keeps Rising from an Unquiet Grave*, N.Y. Times (Mar. 21, 2017).

72. *Augustus Van Wyck*, N.Y. Times Magazine (Oct. 9, 1898).

73. *Holland Society Meeting: Mayor Van Wyck Is Elected President and He Makes a Short Address*, N.Y. Times (Apr. 7, 1898).

74. *Mr. Croker's Methods as Tammany Leader*, N.Y. Times (Dec. 23, 1900).

75. Norman Thomas and Paul Blanchard, What's the Matter with New York 12 (1932).

76. *The Triumph of Tammany*, N.Y. Times (Nov. 4, 1903).

77. *The Biggest Steal of All*, N.Y. Times (Aug. 19, 1899).

78. M.R. Werner, Tammany Hall (1932).

79. *"Big Bill" Devery Dies of Apoplexy*, N.Y. Times (Jun. 21, 1919).

80. *Robert A. Van Wyck Dies in Paris Home*, N.Y. Times (Nov. 15, 1918).

81. *Opening Set Today for 3 Road Links*, N.Y. Times (Oct. 14, 1950).

82. *Id.*

83. Caro, supra note 2 at 910.

84. Nick Paumgarten, *The Van Wyck Question*, New Yorker (Jun. 11, 2001).

85. *Letter from Robert Moses to Andrew W. Mulrain, Commissioner of Sanitation Thanking the Sanitation Department Band for Playing at the Opening Ceremonies of the Van Wyck Expressway* (October 18, 1950).

86. *Id.*

87. Queens Transit Activists, *JFK Airport Express: A Study of the Reactivation of the Long Island Railroad Rockaway Beach Branch* 4 (2013).

88. *Van Wyck Expressway Capacity and Access Improvements to JFK Airport Project DEIS* 2.2.2.1 (2018).

89. Wil Haygood, King of the Cats: The Life and Times of Adam Clayton Powell, Jr. (1993).

90. *Prominent Colored Preacher Tells Students That Negro and White Must Seek to Eliminate Friction*, Colgate Maroon (May 25, 1927).

91. Emily Jeffres and Natalie Sportelli, *Adam Clayton Powell Jr., Class of 1930* (2015), 200. colgate.edu/looking-back/people/adam-clayton-powell-jr-class-1930.

92. *Isabel Washington Powell, 98, Worked with Harlem Students, Prized Vineyard*, Vineyard Gazette (May 3, 2007).

93. Wil Haygood, *Power and Love*, Wash. Post (Jan. 17, 1993).

94. Brown v. Board of Education, 347 U.S. 483 (1954); Charles V. Hamilton, Adam Clayton Powell Jr.: The Political Biography of an American Dilemma (1991).

95. John D. Morris, *Powell Is Punched by House Colleague*, N.Y. Times (Jul. 20, 1955).

96. *Id.*

97. ADAM CLAYTON POWELL JR., ADAM BY ADAM: THE AUTOBIOGRAPHY OF ADAM CLAYTON POWELL 73 (1971).

98. 91 CONG. REC. 1045 (Feb. 13, 1945). During the Second World War, Rankin gave fifty antisemitic speeches in the House. Alfred Friendly, *Jefferson and Rankin*, WASH. POST (Apr. 14, 1947).

99. *Id.*

100. 95 CONG. REC. 13124 (Sept. 21, 1949). (Nb: The congressional record incorrectly reflects Rankin's speech, sanitizing the racial epithets that he used.)

101. HAYGOOD, KING OF THE CATS, *supra* note 93.

102. *Truman Condemns DAR Negro Ban but Wife Attends Tea*, N.Y. TIMES (Oct. 12, 1945); Albin Krebs, *Bess Truman Dead at 97: Was President's Full Partner*, N.Y. TIMES (Oct. 19, 1982).

103. *Fighter for Civil Rights: Adam Clayton Powel, Jr.*, N.Y. TIMES (Jul. 3, 1955).

104. Powell v. McCormack, 395 U.S. 486 (1969).

Part II

105. HOWARD FAST, GOETHALS AND THE PANAMA CANAL (1942).

106. *Goethals, Canal Builder—a Brooklyn Boy*, BROOKLYN DAILY EAGLE (Oct. 12, 1913).

107. *General Goethals Dies Here After Weeks of Illness*, BROOKLYN DAILY EAGLE (Jan. 22, 1928).

108. DONALD DAVIDSON, THE TENNESSEE: THE NEW RIVER 168 (1992).

109. George W. Cullum, *George W. Goethals*, BIOGRAPHICAL REGISTER OF OFFICERS AND GRADUATES OF THE U.S. MILITARY ACADEMY AT WEST POINT 328 (1891).

110. Report of the Board of Consulting Engineers for the Panama Canal (1906).

111. An Act to Provide for Recognition of Certain Officers of the Army, Navy, and Public Health Service for their Services in Connection with the Construction of the Panama Canal, P.L. 316, 63rd Cong. (Mar. 4, 1915).

112. Hearing Before the Sen. Subcomm. on Interocean Canals, 64th Cong. 247 (Mar. 17, 1916) (statement of General Goethals).

113. *Gen. Goethals Dies after Long Illness*, N.Y. TIMES (Jan. 22, 1928).

114. *Expects Goethals Here by September*, BROOKLYN DAILY EAGLE (Feb. 20, 1914).

115. *Police Will Oppose Charter Amendment*, BROOKLYN DAILY EAGLE (Jan. 24, 1914).

116. ROBERT W. JACKSON, TUNNEL UNDER THE HUDSON 34 (2013).

117. Major Roy A. Shane, *Two Acting Quartermasters General and their Assistant*, THE QUARTERMASTER REV. (Sept–Oct. 1951).

118. Erna Risch, QUARTERMASTER SUPPORT OF THE ARMY: A HISTORY OF THE CORPS 1775–1939 633 (1962).

119. Bill Hutchinson, *New $1.5 Billion Goethals Bridge Will Provide Pedestrian, Bike Paths to N.J.*, N.Y. DAILY NEWS (Apr. 25, 2011).

120. GARY NASH AND GRAHAM RUSSELL GAO HODGES, FRIENDS OF LIBERTY (2008).

121. Thaddeus Kościuszko National Memorial, www.ushistory.org/tour/kosciuszko. htm.

122. Amy Cohen, *Revolutionary War Hero Thaddeus Kościuszko Ages Well in New Era of Social Justice*, HIDDEN CITY (Aug. 24, 2020).

123. Will of Tadeusz Kościuszko, 5 May 1798.

124. Armstrong v. Lear, 25 U.S. (12 Wheat.) 169 (1827); Estho v. Lear, 32 U.S. 130 (7 Pet.) 130 (1832); Ennis v. Smith, 55 U.S. (14 How.) 400 (1852).

125. Louis Ottenberg, *A Testamentary Tragedy: Jefferson and the Wills of Kościuszko*, 44 ABA J. 22, 23 (Jan. 1958).

126. Jarosław Czubaty, *A Republican in a Changing World: The Political Position and Attitudes of Tadeusz Kościuszko, 1798–1817*, 59 POLISH REV. 73, 75 (2014).

127. *Kościuszko Bridge Is Named by Mayor*, N.Y. TIMES (Sept. 23, 1940).

128. *Id.*

129. Joint Resolution Proclaiming Pulaski to Be an Honorary Citizen of the United States, P.L. 111-94, 111th Congress (Nov. 6, 2009).

130. *Id.*

131. Henry Wadsworth Longfellow, *Hymn of the Moravian Nuns of Bethlehem at the Consecration of Pulaski's Banner* (1840).

132. Frank A. Reddan, *A Super-Highway System Being Supplemented by a Super Viaduct*, 147 SCI. AM. 83 (1932).

133. American Institute of Steel Construction, *Prize Bridges 1928–1956.*

134. ROBERT W. JACKSON, HIGHWAY UNDER THE HUDSON 33–34 (2013).

135. The New York Harbor Case, 47 I.C.C. 643 (1917).

136. JAMESON, W. DOIG, EMPIRE ON THE HUDSON 58–65 (2002).

137. New York, New Jersey Port and Harbor Development Commission: Joint Report with Comprehensive Plan and Recommendations (1920).

138. New York Code, Port of New York Authority 154/21.

139. *April Supplement*, 11 N.Y. CHAMBER OF COMMERCE MONTHLY BULL. 25 (1921).

140. The New York Red Book 310 (1921).

141. *Port Board Begins Campaign on Radio*, N.Y. TIMES (Jan. 24, 1929).

142. *Port Plan Calls for Two Trunk Lines*, N.Y. TIMES (Nov. 8, 1923).

143. *ICC Order s Aid to Port Authority*, N.Y. TIMES (Dec. 18, 1922).

144. *E.H. Outerbridge Warns of Action by Congress to End Squabbling*, N.Y. HERALD (Jan. 4, 1922).

145. *Penn. Road Drops Potato Embargo*, N.Y. TIMES (Jun. 6, 1922).

146. *Form Syndicate to Bring Coal Here*, N.Y. TIMES (Aug. 10, 1922); JEREMY BRECHER, STRIKE! (1972).

147. *E.H. Outerbridge Seriously Ill*, N.Y. TIMES (Aug. 22, 1922).

148. *A Useful Citizen*, N.Y. TIMES (Mar. 29, 1924).

149. Seymour Freegood, *New Strength in City Hall*, THE EXPLODING METROPOLIS 100–101 (William H. Whyte, ed. 1959).

150. *Congress and the Port Authority of New York: Federal Supervision of Interstate Compacts*, 70 Yale L.J. 812 n.3 (1961).

151. Matthew Arco, *'Time for Some Traffic Problems in Ft. Lee,' Christie Senior Staffer Writes*, Observer (Jan. 8, 2014).

152. Kelly v. United States, 140 S. Ct. 1565 (May 7, 2020).

153. *New Jersey Spans Ahead of Schedule*, N.Y. Times (Jul. 29, 1927).

154. *Arthur Kill Spans Show Rising Income*, N.Y. Times (Jan. 13, 1930).

155. *Bridges and Tubes Gained*, N.Y. Times (Feb. 4, 1931).

156. *Bridge Across Kill van Kull Another Link in Port Unity* (Nov. 8, 1931).

157. Port Authority of New York and New Jersey, 2021 Monthly Traffic and Percent of E-Z Pass Usage, www.panynj.gov/bridges-tunnels/en/traffic---volume-information---b-t.html.

158. Stephen Jenkins, The Story of the Bronx from the Purchase Made by the Dutch in 1639 to the Present Day 197 (1912).

159. Treaty of New York with the Seven Nations of Canada, 7 Stat. 55 (May 31, 1796).

160. Annual Report of the Forest Commission of the State of New York, Vol. 1 79–84 (1894).

161. David J. Cowen, *The First Bank of the United States and the Securities Market Crash of 1792*, 60 J. Econ. Hist. 1041, 1053 (2000).

162. *In Chancery: Samuel Corp, John F. Ellis and Gabriel Shaw vs Alexander Macomb*, N.Y. Evening Post (Jun. 23, 1810).

163. *Id.*

164. *In Chancery: Samuel Corp, John F. Ellis and Gabriel Shaw vs Alexander Macomb*, N.Y. Evening Post (Jan. 4, 1811).

165. Letter from Alexander Hamilton, Inspector General of the U.S. Army, to Secretary of War James McHenry (May 15, 1799).

166. Memoirs of Alexander Macomb, 25–28 (1833).

167. *The Late Major General Macomb*, Spirit of the Times (Jul. 5, 1841).

168. Appendix to the History of the Thirteenth Congress, 28 Annals of Cong. 1964.1965 (1814–1815).

169. *The Army*, Troy Sentinel (Jun. 17, 1828).

170. Committee on Claims Report on Alexander Macomb, 25th Cong, 2nd Sess. Rep. No. 8 (Feb. 4, 1836).

171. *Death of General Macomb*, Delaware Gazette (Jul. 7, 1841).

172. *Mr. Macomb's Appeal Continued*, N.Y. Evening Post (Aug. 12, 1817).

173. *Mr. Macomb's Appeal*, N.Y. Evening Post (Aug. 11, 1817).

174. *Mr. Macomb's Appeal, Concluded*, N.Y. Evening Post (Aug. 13, 1817).

175. *Untitled*, Geneva Gazette (Nov. 11, 1818).

176. Laws of New York, 36th Legislature (1813) Vol. 1 237–238.

177. City of New York v. Campbell, 18 Barb. 156 (Jun. 1, 1854).

178. Campbell v. Macomb, 4 Johns Ch. 534 (1820).

179. City of New York Common Council Minutes 81–88 (March 1817).

180. A Demand to Get Through Macomb's Dam and Coles' Bridge, by Schooner Superior, Captain Marshall (1838), *reproduced in* Harlaem River: Its Use Previous to and Since the Revolutionary War And Suggestions Relative to Present Contemplated Improvement (1857).

181. Renwick v. Morris, 3 Hill 621 (1842).

182. Mayor of New York v. Campbell, 18 Barb. 156 (Jun. 1, 1854).

183. Laws of New York, 81st Legislature (1858) 452–456.

184. *Macomb's Dam Park Saved*, N.Y. Times (Apr. 9, 1918).

185. *Twin Tubes Under Hudson Will Care for Future Traffic*, The Sun and N.Y. Herald (Feb. 22, 1920).

186. *New York–Jersey Tunnel Proposed before Congress*, Evening World (Jun. 28, 1918).

187. *No Coal Coming into City Today: Crisis at Its Worst*, Evening World (Dec. 31, 1917).

188. Michael Aronson, *The Digger Clifford Holland*, Daily News (Jun. 15, 1999).

189. Robert G. Skerrett, *Driving with Air the Hudson Vehicular Twin Tubes*, 25 Compressed Air 9741, 9743–4 (Aug. 1920).

190. *Vehicle Tunnel Bill Passed by Assembly*, Evening World (Feb. 26, 1919).

191. *World's Greatest Auto Tunnel Started*, New Britain Herald (Jun. 21, 1922).

192. *New York Vehicular Tunnels Teach Valuable Traffic Lessons*, The Sunday Star (Dec. 4, 1927).

193. American Society of Civil Engineers, *Holland Tunnel*, www.ascemetsection.org/committees/history-and-heritage/landmarks/holland-tunnel.

194. *Work Begins Today on Jersey Tunnel*, N.Y. Times (Mar. 31, 1922).

195. *A Tribute to Engineer: Vehicular Tunnel Will Be Named after C.M. Holland Who Designed It*, N.Y. Times (Mar. 22, 1925).

196. *Holland Tunnel*, Time (Nov. 21, 1927).

197. *Great Crowd Treks into Holland Tubes after Gala Opening*, N.Y. Times (Nov. 13, 1927).

198. Helena Fox, *Holland Tunnel Opens to the Public*, Daily News (Nov. 13, 1927).

199. *To Walk Under Hudson*, Evening World (Jun. 22, 1918).

200. Skerrett, supra note 205 at 9745.

201. *Holland Tube Roadways Involve a Huge Task*, N.Y. Times (Aug. 21, 1927).

202. *Toll Scale Is Fixed for Holland Tunnel*, N.Y. Times (Nov. 2, 1927).

203. *Toll Rates for All Port Authority Bridge and Tunnels* (2022), www.panynj.gov/bridges-tunnels/tolls.html.

Part III

204. Jan Albers, Sylvia and Charity: a Vermont Love Story for the Ages (2015).

205. *Editorial*, Evening Post (Mar. 9, 1857).

206. Gilbert H. Muller, William Cullen Bryant: Author of America 241(2010).

207. ALLAN NEVINS, THE EVENING POST: A CENTURY OF JOURNALISM 250 (1922).

208. *Republicans at Cooper Union; Address by Hon. Abraham Lincoln, of Illinois. Remarks by Messrs. Wm. Cullen Bryant, Horace Greeley, Gen. Nye and J.A. Briggs*, N.Y. TIMES (Feb. 28, 1860).

209. *Gen. Lane, His Address Before the Emancipation League*, N.Y. TIMES (Jun. 6, 1861).

210. An Act to Incorporate the Freedman's Savings and Trust Company (Mar. 3, 1865).

211. *The Birthday of Burns. Centennial Anniversary*, N.Y. TIMES (Jan. 26, 1859).

212. *Mr Bryant Worse*, N.Y. TIMES (Jun. 11, 1878); *City and Suburban News: New York*, N.Y. TIMES (Jun. 9, 1878); *Mr William Cullen Bryant's Illness*, N.Y. TIMES (Jun. 4, 1878).

213. *Thanatopsis Realized*, N.Y. TIMES (Jun. 13, 1878).

214. *Mr. Bryant's Funeral*, N.Y. TIMES (Jun. 15, 1878).

215. *Shirley Chisholm Is Wed to Buffalo Merchant*, N.Y. TIMES (Nov. 27, 1977).

216. Julie Gallagher, *Waging the Good Fight: The Political Career of Shirley Chisholm 1952–1982*, 97 J. AF. AM. HIST. 392, 398 (2007).

217. Susan Brownmiller, *This Is Fighting Shirley Chisholm*, N.Y. TIMES (Apr. 13, 1969).

218. WAYNE DAWKINS, CITY SON: ANDREW W. COOPER'S IMPACT ON MODERN-DAY BROOKLYN (2012).

219. John Kifner, *Farmer and Woman in Lively Bedford-Stuyvesant Race*, N.Y. TIMES (Oct. 26, 1968).

220. *Id.*

221. Office of the Historian, *A Changing of the Guard* 327, in WOMEN IN CONGRESS 1917–2020, H. Doc 116-152 (2020) (quoting former representative Catherine Dean May).

222. Richard L. Madden, *Mrs. Chisholm Gets Off House Farm Committee*, N.Y. TIMES (Jan. 29, 1969).

223. *Id.*

224. *Id.*

225. *Mrs. Chisholm Is Elected to a Veteran's Committee*, N.Y. TIMES (Feb. 19, 1969).

226. JOSEPH TELUSHKIN, THE LIFE AND TEACHINGS OF MENACHEM M. SCHNEERSON, THE MOST INFLUENTIAL RABBI IN MODERN HISTORY 13–15 (2014).

227. Carlyle C. Douglas and Richard Levine, *Shirley Chisholm Calls It a Day*, N.Y. TIMES (Feb. 14, 1982).

228. Charlayne Hunter, *Shirley Chisholm: Willing to Speak Out*, N.Y. TIMES (May 22, 1970).

229. Jillian Steinhauer, *The Shirley Chisholm Monument in Brooklyn Finds Its Designers*, N.Y. TIMES (Apr. 23, 2019).

230. BILLIE JEAN KING, ALL IN 412 (2021).

231. Emily Bobrow, *Tennis Legend Billie Jean King Transformed the Game*, WALL ST. J. (Aug. 13, 2021).

232. Melissa Murphy, *"We Risked Our Careers": Original 9 Mark 50 Years of Women's Pro Tennis Circuit*, CBC.CA (Sept. 6, 2020).

233. Emily Bobrow, *Tennis Legend Billie Jean King Transformed the Game*, Wall St. J. (Aug. 13, 2021).

234. *About the WTA*, WTATennis.com (undated).

235. *Original 9 Secure Hall of Fame Status*, WTA News (Feb. 24, 2021).

236. Don Van Natta Jr., *The Match Maker*, ESPN.com (Mar. 26, 2020).

237. Neil Amdur, *Discussed and Dissected, Billie Jean, Bobby Ready*, N.Y. Times (Sept. 20, 1973).

238. Neil Amdur, *"She Played Too Well," Says Riggs of King*, N.Y. Times (Sept. 22, 1973).

239. Anna Diamond, *The True Story Behind Billie Jean King's Victorious "Battle of the Sexes,"* Smithsonian (Sept. 22, 2107).

240. Jake Curtis, *Ranking the Greatest Champions in Wimbledon History*, Bleacher Report (Jul. 1, 2015).

241. *Billie Jean King Leadership Initiative, Vision*, bjkli.org.

242. *Billie Jean King Youth Leadership Award*, ESPN.com (Jul. 15, 2021).

243. William Alfred Shea, Prabook, prabook.com/web/person-view. html?profileId=60717.

244. Nicholas Pileggi, *No Matter Who Loses the Election, Bill Shea Wins*, New York Magazine (1974).

245. Jack Newfield and Paul DuBrul, The Permanent Government (1983).

246. Michael Shapiro, Bottom of the Ninth: Branch Rickey, Casey Stengel, and the Daring Scheme to Save Baseball from Itself (2009).

247. Bill Morales, Farewell to the Last Golden Era: The Yankees, the Pirates and the 1960 Baseball Season (2011).

248. Jan Hoffman, *An End to a Lawfirm That Defined a Type*, N.Y. Times (Feb. 7, 1994).

249. *Id.*

250. *Id.*

251. Eric Pooley, *The Firm*, New York (February 21, 1994).

252. Newfield and DuBrul, *supra* n. 275.

253. Dedication: William A. Shea Municipal Stadium, www.worldsfairphotos.com/ nywf64/booklets/shea-dedication-4-16-64.pdf.

254. George Vecsey, *A Bitter Acceptance as Mets Fall*, N.Y. Times (Sept. 28, 2008).

255. *Texas News*, The Jewish Herald (Dec. 30, 1909).

256. Natalie Ornish, Pioneer Jewish Texans 97–98 (2011).

257. *Albert Lasker*, Immigrant Entrepreneurship.org.

258. Jeffrey L. Cruikshank and Arthur W. Schultz, The Man Who Sold America (2010).

259. *Ellis Island Looks to Care for Guests*, N.Y. Herald (Jan. 3, 1922).

260. CHPC New York, *History*, chpcny.org/about-us/history.

261. Loula D. Lasker, *Putting a White Collar on the East Side*, THE SURVEY (Mar. 13, 1931).

262. *Urban League '51 Drive Opens in New York*, MIAMI TIMES (Apr. 21, 1951).

263. *Scholarships for Housing Study Provided in Miss Lasker's Will*, N.Y. TIMES (March 14, 1961).

264. *Four UNCF Students Awarded Lasker Fellowships*, JACKSON ADVOC. (Jun. 2, 1962).

265. NORVAL WHITE, ELLIOT WILLENSKY, FRAN LEADON, AIA GUIDE TO NEW YORK CITY 414 (2000).

Part IV

266. ERIC JAY DOLAN, FUR, FORTUNE AND EMPIRE 190 (2010).

267. EDWIN G. BURROWS AND MIKE WALLACE, GOTHAM: A HISTORY OF NEW YORK CITY TO 1898 273 (1999).

268. WASHINGTON IRVING, ASTORIA: ON ENTERPRISE BEYOND THE ROCKY MOUNTAINS (1836).

269. ALEXANDER EMMERICH, JOHN JACOB ASTOR 47–48 (2009).

270. An Act to Incorporate the American Fur Company (April 6, 1808).

271. John D. Haeger, *Business Strategy and Practice in the Early Republic: John Jacob Astor and the American Fur Trade*, 19 WESTERN HISTORICAL Q. 183, 189 (May 1988).

272. *Thomas Jefferson to John Jacob Astor* (April 13, 1808) in JEFFERSON, THE WRITINGS OF THOMAS JEFFERSON, vol. 11, 28.

273. IRVING, *supra* note 299.

274. ARTHUR D. HOWDEN SMITH, JOHN JACOB ASTOR: LANDLORD OF NEW YORK 97 (1929).

275. Dolan, *supra* note 297 at 194.

276. *Millionaires of New York*, N.Y. TIMES (Dec. 26, 1878).

277. *The All-Time Richest Americans*, FORBES (Sept. 14, 2007).

278. Christopher Grey, *Where Lincoln Tossed and Turned*, N.Y. TIMES (Sept. 24, 2009).

279. Barbara Foley, *From Wall Street to Astor Place: Historicizing Melville's Bartelby*, 72 AM. LIT. 87 (2000).

280. Stephen Zelnick, *Melville's Bartelby: History, Ideology and Literature*, 2 MARXIST PERSP. 75 (Winter 1979–80).

281. JAMES PARTON, LIFE OF JOHN JACOB ASTOR (1865); Harry Miller Lydenberg, *History of the New York Public Library*, 20 BULL. N.Y. PUB. LIBR. 555, 557, 566 (1916).

282. *Id.* at 559.

283. Christopher Grey, *Streetscape?: The Old Astor Library, Now the Joseph Papp Public Theatre; Once It Held Many Pages; Now It Has Many Stages*, N.Y. TIMES (Feb. 10, 2002).

284. Lydenberg, *supra* note 312 at 651.

285. Richard F. Shepard, *Papp's Troupe Gets 1850's Landmark for Indoor Home*, N.Y. TIMES (Jan. 6, 1966).

286. *Astor's Family Are to Divide $100,000,000*, L.A. HERALD (Apr. 18, 1912).

287. John Richardson, *The Battle for Mrs. Astor*, VANITY FAIR (Oct. 2008).

288. CALENDAR OF HISTORICAL MANUSCRIPTS, PART 1, DUTCH MANUSCRIPTS 1630–1664 at 366 (Edmund Bailey O'Callaghan ed. 1865–1866).

289. *Id.* at 24–25.

290. *Id.* at 366.

291. REGINALD PELHAM BOLTON, INDIAN PATHS IN THE GREAT METROPOLIS 144 (1922).

292. JOSEPH ALEXIU, GOWANUS: BROOKLYN'S CURIOUS CANAL 27 (2015).

293. BOLTON, INDIAN PATHS, *supra* note 322 144 (1922).

294. ALEXIU, *supra* note 323 at 27–29.

295. MARK KURLANSKY, THE BIG OYSTER (2006).

296. Allison Smith, *Could New York's "Black Mayonnaise" Problem Sink a New 82-Block Development?* THE GUARDIAN (Sept. 2, 2021).

297. Jeanne Toomey, *Our Lavender Lake Is a Busy Ditch*, BROOKLYN DAILY EAGLE (Jun. 22, 1952).

298. This remains true. Jaime DeJesus, *Body Found in Gowanus Canal*, BROOKLYN REPORTER (Sept. 3, 2021); Jen Chung, *Body Found in Gowanus Canal Deemed a Homicide*, GOTHAMIST (Jun. 7, 2018); Kristen Iverson, *Dead Body Found Floating in Gowanus Canal This Afternoon*, BK MAG. (Apr. 21, 2014). The list goes on.

299. Edward Lewine, *The Gowanus Canal: An Appreciation*, N.Y. TIMES (Aug. 30, 1998).

300. Superfund Site: Gowanus Canal, Brooklyn, NY, cumulis.epa.gov/supercpad/SiteProfiles/index.cfm?fuseaction=second.cleanup&id=0206222.

301. Leslie Albrecht, *Anticipated Development Drives Record Sale of Gowanus Empty Lot*, DNAINFO (Mar. 29, 2016).

302. Adriaen van der Donck, DESCRIPTION OF NEW NETHERLANDS AS IT IS TODAY (1655).

303. Adriaen van der Donck, *Remonstrance of New Netherland and Occurrences There* (1856).

304. Van Rensselaer Bowier Manuscripts, Being the Letters of Killiaen Van Rensselaer 1630–1643 at 538.

305. BERTHOLD FERNOW, DOCUMENTS RELATIVE TO THE COLONIAL HISTORY OF THE STATE OF NEW YORK 111–114 (1883).

306. *Id.*

307. *Id.* at 50–51. Adriaen van der Donck, *supra* note 337 at 48, 63.

308. *Id.*

309. *Id.* at 39.

310. *Resolution of the States General, Recalling Governor Stuyvesant*, in Fernow, *supra* note 339 at 471–472.

311. *Resolution of the States General Revoking the Recall of Governor Stuyvesant*, in Fernow, *supra* note 339 at 475.

312. DESCRIPTION OF NEW NETHERLANDS, *supra* note 336 at 1.

313. Ada van Gastel, *Van der Donck's Description of the Indians: Additions and Corrections,*47 WM. AND MARY Q. 411, 412 (July 1990).

314. *Resolution of the States General Granting Copyright to Adriaen van der Donck*, in Fernow, *supra* note 339 at 533.

315. THE STAFFORDSHIRE POTTERIES DIRECTORY FOR 1868.

316. *Job and John Jackson*, Printed British Pottery and Porcelain 1750–1900 printedbritishpotteryandporcelain.com/who-made-it/jackson-maker.

317. NEW YORK SPECTATOR (Feb. 18, 1831).

318. J and J Jackson Platter, circa 1831, www.metmuseum.org/art/collection/search/192988.

319. GEORGE ELWICK, THE BANKRUPTCY DIRECTORY 223 (1843).

320. *Obituary*, N.Y. TIMES (Sept. 19, 1899).

321. CHARLES ARTHUR CONANT, THE PROGRESS OF THE EMPIRE STATE: A WORK DEVOTED TO THE HISTORICAL, FINANCIAL, INDUSTRIAL, AND LITERARY DEVELOPMENT OF NEW YORK 315 (1913).

322. MUNSELL, *supra* note 357 at 317.

323. *Long Island Trains,* JAMAICA FARMER (May 18, 1871).

324. Shelley v. Kraemer, 334 U.S. 1 (1948).

325. David Anthony Schmidt, *Princeton Seminary and Slavery, Appendix B: Financial History 1811–1861,* slavery.ptsem.edu/the-report/appendix-b.

326. Robert Lenox, *Advertisement*, THE EVENING POST (Jul. 28, 1817).

327. *New York Millionaires*, N.Y. TIMES (Dec. 26, 1878).

328. *One of the People*, THE [NEW YORK] ARGUS, OR GREENLEAF'S NEW DAILY ADVERTISER (Dec. 25, 1795).

329. MARY LOUISE BOOTH, THE HISTORY OF NEW YORK, Vol. 1 512 (1854); Philip Ranlet, *Tory David Sproat of Pennsylvania and the Death of American Prisoners of War*, 61 PA. HIST. 185, 190 (Apr. 1994).

330. THE [NEW YORK] ARGUS, OR GREENLEAF'S NEW DAILY ADVERTISER (Dec. 28, 1795).

331. Alexander Hamilton, *Certificate on Robert Lenox* (Jan. 11, 1796).

332. William Wirt Philips, *Address Delivered in the First Presbyterian Church, New York, at the Funeral of Robert Lenox, Esq.* (Dec. 16, 1839).

333. *Id.*

334. *My Farm at the Five Mile Stone*, THE GALAXY, Vol. 19 at 479–81 (William Conant Church, ed, Apr. 1875).

335. *Death of James Lenox: The End of a Philanthropic Life*, N.Y. TIMES (Feb. 19, 1880).

336. HENRY STEVENS, RECOLLECTIONS OF MR. JAMES LENOX OF NEW YORK AND THE FORMATION OF HIS LIBRARY 2 (1886).

337. *Id.* at 118–127.

338. Paul Grodinger, *Architecture: Two Richard Morris Hunt Shows*, N.Y. TIMES (May 26, 1988).

339. BULL. N.Y. PUB. LIBR. 685 (Sept. 1916).

340. BERTHOLD FERNOW, THE RECORDS OF NEW AMSTERDAM 1–8 (1897) (translated by Edmund B. O'Callighan).

341. FREDERICK ROBERTSON JONES, THE HISTORY OF NORTH AMERICA: THE COLONIZATION OF THE MIDDLE STATES AND MARYLAND 36–37, 121–124, 128–130 (1904).

342. van der Donck, *Remonstrance, supra* note 337.

343. *Resolution Recalling Stuyvesant,* Fernow, *supra* note 339 at 471–472.

344. *Id.* at 475.

345. Andrea Mosterman, *The Slave Ship Gideon and the African Captives It Transported to New Netherland,* New Netherlands Institute (undated).

346. Lee E. Cooper, *Uprooted Thousands Start Trek from Site of Stuyvesant Town,* N.Y. TIMES (Mar. 3, 1945).

347. Dorsey v. Stuyvesant Town, 299 N.Y. 512.

348. *Stuyvesant Town to Admit Negros after a Controversy of Seven Years,* N.Y. TIMES (Aug. 25, 1950).

349. *Writ Denied to Tenants,* N.Y. Times (Feb. 14, 1951); *Stuyvesant Town Drops Evictions as Halley Intervenes as Mediator,* N.Y. TIMES (Jan. 21, 1952).

350. Gabriel Sherman, *The Biggest, Baddest Real Estate Loan,* NEW YORK (Dec. 18, 2009).

351. Roberts v. Tishman Speyer, 13 N.Y. 3d. (2009).

352. *Vintage Postcards of Bayside,* Bayside Historical Society, www.baysidehistorical.org/vintage-postcards/Shore-Acres.

353. New York City Landmarks Preservation Commission, Fort Totten Historic District Designation Report 4 (June 1999).

354. *Military and Civil Law Conflict,* N.Y TIMES (Apr. 21, 1895).

355. Sarah Maslin Nir, *Until an Ancestral Graveyard Is Found, No Time to Rest,* N.Y TIMES (Jun. 1, 2012).

356. MUNSELL, *supra* note 357 at 75–79.

357. House of Representatives, *Wilkins' or Willetts Point Investigation,* H.R. Rep. No. 549 at 14 (Jun. 8, 1858).

358. *The Willets Point Investigation,* N.Y. TIMES (Jun. 4, 1858).

359. *Willetts Point Investigation, supra* note 399 at 2.

360. *Id.*

361. House of Representatives, *Report from the Committee on Private Land Claims,* H.R. Rep. No. 460 at 379 (May 29, 1858) (memorandum from William W. Valk).

362. *Fort Totten at Willets Point,* N.Y. TIMES (Jul. 29, 1898).

363. Jodi Wilgoren, *An Old Fort's Last Protector; Veteran Keeps Fort Totten, an Army Relic, from Fading Away,* N.Y. TIMES (Jul. 16, 1999).

364. Avella v. City of New York, 29 N.Y.3d 425, 427 (2017).

365. *Site in Queens Urged by Moses for Park to Remain a Junkyard,* N.Y. TIMES (Jun. 11, 1967).

366. Anahad O'Conner and Terry Pristin, *Bloomberg Unveils Plan to Redevelop Willets Point*, N.Y. Times (May 1, 2007).

367. The Iron Triangle, theirontrianglemovie.com.

Part V

368. B.H. Friedman, Gertrude Vanderbilt Whitney: A Biography 1 (1978).

369. Whitney Museum, Gertrude Whitney Memorial Exhibit 1 (1943), archive.org/details/memorialexhibiti00whit/page/n3/mode/2up.

370. Topeka Daily Capital (Jul. 28, 1907).

371. *Retracing the Spanish Path of My Ancestor*, N.Y. Times (Oct. 9, 2019).

372. *Mrs. H.P. Whitney Wins*, N.Y. Times (Jan. 8, 1914).

373. Gertrude Whitney Papers, Box_0001m Folder 007, available online at edan.si.edu/slideshow/viewer/?damspath=/CollectionsOnline/whitgert/Box_0001/Folder_007.

374. *Id.*

375. *Id.*

376. *Gloria's Mother May Lose $1,000-a-Month Allowance*, Pittsburgh Press (Nov. 23, 1934).

377. *Gloria Vanderbilt Is Ward of Court*, Lewiston Daily Sun (Nov. 21, 1934).

378. Native-lands.ca.; Benjamin Franklin Thompson, History of Long Island: Containing an Account of the Discovery and Settlement: With Other Important and Interesting Matters to the Present Time 410 (1930).

379. James Riker, A Brief History of the Rikers from Their Immigration to the Present Day (1851).

380. Rev. J. Howard Suydam, Hendrick Rycken: The Progenitor of the Suydam Family in America 25 (1898).

381. *Samuel Riker*, history.house.gov/People/Detail/20403.

382. Rocellus Sheridan Guernsey, New York City and Vicinity During the War of 1812, 123 (1889).

383. *Domestic News*, Virginia Argus (Sept. 3, 1812) (reporting the August 28 launch of the *Saratoga*).

384. George Foster Emmons, The Navy of the United States, From the Commencement, 1775 to 1853 192 (1850).

385. *Domestic News*, Alexandria Gazette Commercial and Political (Oct. 19, 1812).

386. *Letter from British Commodore Beresford to British Admiral Sir John Warren, July 7, 1813*, The Gazette (Oct. 12–16, 1813).

387. U.S. Navy, The Naval War of 1812 Vol. II at 281 (1992).

388. Cuyler Reynolds, Genealogy and Family History of Southern New York and the Hudson River Valley, Vol. II. 730 (1914).

389. *Memories of Lafayette*, N.Y. TIMES (Oct. 14. 1900).

390. Harry B. Yoshpe, *Record of Slave Manumissions in New York During the Colonial and Early National Periods* 26 J. NEGRO HISTORY 78–107 (1941).

391. Brentin Mock, *The Dark "Fugitive Slave" History of Rikers Island*, BLOOMBERG CITYLAB (Jul. 23, 2015).

392. Black Abolitionist Papers Vol. 3 at 180 (C. Peter Ripley, ed. 1985).

393. David Ruggles, *Kidnapping in the City of New York*, THE LIBERATOR (Aug. 6, 1836); ERIC FONER, GATEWAY TO FREEDOM: THE HIDDEN HISTORY OF THE UNDERGROUND RAILROAD (2015); BURROWS AND WALLACE, *supra* note 298 at 491–92.

394. Ruggles, *supra* note 438.

395. Will Di Novi, *Re-Naming Rikers*, PAC. STANDARD (Jun. 14, 2017) (quoting historian Jacob Morris).

396. *City Intelligence*, N.Y. TIMES (Apr. 26, 1860).

397. BENSON J. LOSSING, HISTORY OF NEW YORK 240 (1884).

398. *Id.*

399. *An Act to Provide for the Purchase of the Island Known as Rikers*, 1884 Laws of New York 328.

400. U.S. Department of Justice, CRIPA Investigation of the New York Department of Correction Jails on Rikers Island 3 (2014).

401. WILLIAM H. BROWN, THE HISTORY OF THE FIRST LOCOMOTIVES IN AMERICA 107–123 (1891).

402. BURROWS AND WALLACE, *supra* note 298 at 675.

403. *Speech of Abraham Lincoln, of Illinois, Delivered at the Cooper Institute, Monday Feb. 27, 1860*, N.Y. TRIBUNE Tract No. 4 (1860).

404. *Republicans at Cooper Institute: Address by Hon. Abraham Lincoln of Illinois*, N.Y. TIMES (Feb. 28, 1860).

405. *Memorial on Behalf of the Indian Tribes by the United States Indian Commission*, H. Misc. Doc. No. 165, 40th Cong. 2nd Sess. (1868).

406. *Our Indian Visitors*, N.Y. TIMES (Jun. 2, 1871).

407. *Roosevelt and Lehman*, N.Y. TIMES (Oct. 18, 1928).

408. *Lehman Honored by Alma Mater, Williams College*, JEWISH DAILY BULLETIN (Jun. 26, 1929).

409. Robert Alden, *Herbert Lehman, 85, Dies: Ex-Governor and Senator*, N.Y. TIMES (Dec. 6, 1963).

410. *Chinese Honor Lehman*, N.Y. TIMES (Aug. 1, 1947).

411. *Lehman a Leader as Junior Senator*, N.Y. TIMES (Nov. 8, 1950).

412. Warren Moscow, *Deep Issues Involved in Dulles-Lehman Fight*, N.Y. TIMES (Oct. 16, 1949).

413. DUANE TANANBAUM, HERBERT H. LEHMAN: A POLITICAL BIOGRAPHY 337 (2016).

414. Warren Weaver Jr., *Johnson Recalls Lehman Prayer as He Presents Medal to Widow*, N.Y. TIMES (Jan. 29, 1964).

415. *Statement by the President.*

416. *Top Performers on Social Mobility*, US NEWS, www.usnews.com/best-colleges/rankings/regional-universities-north/social-mobility.

417. REV. CHARLES M. SELLACK, NORWALK 174 (1896).

418. *Gracie Mansion to Be Preserved*, N.Y. TIMES (Apr. 2, 1922).

419. *Id.*

420. *Gracie Mansion to Be Preserved*, N.Y. TIMES (Apr. 2, 1922).

421. *My Farm at the Five Mile Stone*, THE GALAXY, Vol. 19 at 473–75 (William Conant Church, ed., Apr. 1875).

422. *Gracie Mansion to Be Preserved*, N.Y. TIMES (Apr. 2, 1922); *Patriotic Society of New Yorkers Formed*, N.Y. TIMES (Dec. 2, 1920).

423. Elisabeth Bumiller, *Giuliani May Leave Mansion to Escape Marital Tensions*, N.Y. TIMES (Jun. 29, 2001).

424. National Register of Historic Places, Nominating Form: Gracie Mansion (May 12, 1975).

425. MELVIN G. HOLLI, THE AMERICAN MAYOR (1993).

426. *LaGuardia Is Dead; City Pays Homage to 3-Time Mayor*, N.Y. TIMES (Sept. 21, 1947).

427. *Id.*

428. ALYN BRODSKY, THE GREAT MAYOR 90 (2003).

429. MASON D. WILLIAMS, CITY OF AMBITION (2014).

430. *Yale Confers 10 Honorary Degrees*, LEWISTON EVENING J. (Jun. 19, 1940). For the full text of the Yale proclamation, *see* H. PAUL JEFFERS, THE NAPOLEON OF NEW YORK: MAYOR FIORELLO LA GUARDIA 243 (2002).

431. John Kalish, *Ravensbrucks's Famous Survivor*, JEWISH DAILY FORWARD (June 26, 2007).

432. *LaGuardia Bier Viewed by 45,000*, N.Y. TIMES (Sept. 22, 1947).

INDEX